PUTTING

THE GAME WITHIN
THE GAME

PUTTING

THE GAME WITHIN THE GAME

CollinsWillow
An Imprint of HarperCollins*Publishers*

First published in 1992 by
Collins Willow
an imprint of HarperCollins Publishers
London

© SP Creative Design 1992

A CIP catalogue for this book is
available from the British Library

ISBN 0 00 218432 X

Designed and produced by SP Creative Design
Linden House, Kings Road, Bury St Edmunds, Suffolk
Art Director: Rolando Ugolini
Editor: Heather Thomas
Production: Laurence Scarlett

Photographs by Rolando Ugolini, Allsport,
Mark Shearman and Yours in Sport

The publishers would like to thank the following
individuals and golf clubs for their help in
creating this book:
Bowood Golf and Country Club, Calne, Wiltshire
Greg Dukart, Head Professional at East Sussex National Golf Club
Les Jones, Golf Professional at Woodbridge Golf Club, Suffolk

Typeset in Stone Serif by Halcyon Type & Design, Ipswich, Suffolk
Colour origination by C.L.G., Verona, Italy

Printed and bound in Italy by New Interlitho SpA, Milan

Contents

Nick Allen

Nick Allen is a PGA professional and consultant with Apollo Golf Shafts, which operates a Tour Support Service on the European Tour. He has played extensively on the professional circuit both in the United States and Europe. He is also the director of a golf course development company.

Alasdair Barr

Alasdair Barr is Director of Golf at Brocket Hall in Hertfordshire. He is both a Senior Swing Instructor and Senior Swing Examiner for the PGA Training School. In 1987 he became the National Coach to the English Golf Union and he also coaches the Berkshire, Buckinghamshire and Oxfordshire Senior, Junior and Ladies County teams.

Nigel Blenkarne

Nigel Blenkarne has 18 years experience as a professional golfer. He became PGA qualified in 1977 and earned his European Tour Players card finishing third behind Sandy Lyle. After three years playing full time in Europe and South Africa, he became club professional at Salisbury, later moving on to the picturesque Parkstone Golf Club in Dorset, and in 1992 was appointed Director of Golf at Bowood Golf and Country Club, Wiltshire.

Nigel's teaching ability has made him well known and sought after, and he coaches a number of successful tournament professionals. He has written and co-presented the video *Golf for Women* with pupil Diane Barnard, a winner on the WPG European Tour, and he has contributed to several golf books.

Craig DeFoy

Craig DeFoy is the golf professional at Coombe Hill Golf Club, Surrey. He was a tournament player on the European circuit for many years and has won several tournaments. He has represented Wales seven times in the World Cup, and Britain twice in the PGA Cup. He is now the Welsh National Coach.

David Johnson

David Johnson is Director of Golf and Head Professional at Little Hay Golf Complex in Hertfordshire. He is one of the few remaining golf club makers still in existence and a Senior Tutor at the PGA Training School. He is a past member of the Tournament Players Division of the PGA and has the reputation of being a fine golf instructor.

Kevin Jones

Kevin Jones is the Golf Professional at Caldy Golf Club in Lancashire. He has won many tournaments including the PGA Cup in 1988 and has been Welsh Professional Champion twice – in 1984 and 1989. He has represented Wales and was the Teaching Professional at Sheko Golf Club in Hong Kong before going to Caldy in 1980.

Les Jones

Les Jones acted as a consultant on this book. He is the Golf Professional at Woodbridge Golf Club, Suffolk. He was Head of the Swing Department for the PGA Tutorial Body from 1989 to 1992, and has been a PGA Swing Instructor for 18 years. He has won the Middlesex Professional Championship and has been Suffolk Open Champion on four consecutive occasions.

Martin Vousden

Martin Vousden is the deputy editor of *Today's Golfer* magazine in the UK. He writes regular features on the Rules of Golf and the international professional circuit for the magazine. His great regret is that he did not take up golf until his late twenties, but he now plays regularly and has a handicap of 12.

CHAPTER ONE

Choosing a putter

by Nigel Blenkarne

With a great many styles and variations of putters available, it is not an easy task to select the most suitable for you. Putting is probably the most mentally influenced part of golf, and that explains why there are more putter designs and options available than any other type of equipment.

The key, of course, is to find the one that works best for you. Successful results breed confidence, which in turn will lead to successful results and so the positive cycle is strengthened. Likewise a negative attitude can produce a spiral of bad results and at this point a change of putter is advisable. The majority of good golfers will have two or three reserve putters to fall back on if their regular old faithful just isn't working; a short spell with a different putter will often set you up for a confident return to a tried and tested one.

You may have a patient personality and adopt the attitude that if a putter has worked well in the past and you have a temporary loss of form that through practice and working on your technique, success will return. However, it requires deep-rooted faith and confidence in the instrument you are using.

Unlike other golf clubs, which have to be fitted to each person, there are really no hard and fast guidelines that need to be adhered to in finding the right putter. It is largely an exercise of trial and error and due to the fact that for an average or better golfer in excess of 40 per cent of shots will be played with the putter it is easy to understand why players change their putter far more than any other club in the bag. Your score will be affected more rapidly than in any other section of the game, negatively or positively, by your performance with the putter.

If you are selecting a putter for the first time or you are thinking of having a change, make sure that you go to a PGA Professional who is prepared to let you try a few putters on a good putting green before you make your final choice. They all look good in the shop but until you have experienced that vital ingredient *feel*, you really cannot compare. In this chapter, we will examine the different factors of which you should be aware when choosing a putter.

Choosing a putter

Head design

It is important that you like the look of your putter head, and this will, in turn, give you enthusiasm and confidence for putting. Early putter designs were all very similar: a flat blade which resembled a long iron, with a shorter shaft and reduced loft (between six and ten degrees). Interestingly, they were often numbered 9 and sold as part of the set of irons when an 8 iron was the most lofted club. In modern times the putter is an individual club and very rarely sold with the other clubs.

Blade putters are still available and popular. One of the world's acknowledged great putters, Ben Crenshaw, uses a blade with a flange (wide sole) but it does demand a very good putting stroke because the sweet spot is not as large as it is on other putters.

Left: A traditional flat blade putter; this one has a hickory shaft.
Above: A blade putter with a flange.

10

Two variations of heel- and toe-weighted putters; on the left are the sighting lines.

Heel and toe weighted putter heads will give you a wider sweet spot that is more forgiving of an off-centre strike. If a putt that would normally travel 20 feet is struck ½ inch from the centre, it will travel only 16 to 18 feet. Putters with good heel and toe weight distribution will hit putts further on off-centre hits than those without, but both types of putter should give the same performance on centre hits.

Mallet putters are shaped in a similar way to wood clubs and have a thick club head from the face to the back. Often they are not solid but have internal heel and toe weighting. Some have a removable soleplate which allows for weight adjustment (eg. the 'Ram Zebra').

This mallet putter is made from wood with a metal insert.

Choosing a putter

The sole design and lie angle must be considered carefully and are influenced by your stance and the distance you wish to stand from the ball. The sole may be either flat or rounded; if it is flat, then the lie angle (the angle at which the shaft comes out of the head) must be correct, otherwise either the toe or heel will snag the ground. A rounded sole allows more variation in the address position because only the centre piece of the sole will be close to the ground. This allows you to hold your hands high or low without fear of the putter head twisting if it catches the ground slightly.

Some sole designs will incorporate sighting lines which you may find useful to aim the putter. It is important that these lines are accurately built in to the head; on some cheaper putters, they are not at 90 degrees to the face of the putter and may not indicate correctly the sweet spot.

This wide triangular design gives a long sighting line.

Head materials used in putters are far more varied than for other golf clubs. Whilst it is difficult to generalize, here is a list of the most widely used materials and how the feel is influenced.

● **Brass** A soft but dense feel. The head must be fairly small if solid brass is used; it is a heavy metal and will dent easily if unprotected.
● **Aluminium/alloy** A light metal which allows for a larger head design. It needs to be well made, not to feel flimsy and rather tinny. It is also quite soft and therefore needs protection.
● **Stainless steel** A hard metal with a positive feel. It will not mark easily so a putter cover is not necessary unless a paint finish is used.
● **Manganese bronze** A hard metal which gives a firm feel. It discolours to a dark bronze with time and does not need protection.
● **Berylium copper** A heavy material, reddish in appearance. Gives a dead feel and is also fairly hard, so there is no need to protect it although it will discolour in time.
● **Mild steel** A soft metal which gives a springy feel and keeps the ball rolling well. It does require looking after and will rust if left wet. It is easily adjusted for a change of lie.

● **Married metal** A brass or mild steel face insert is used in an otherwise different metal to give the benefit of a soft feel with durability.

● **Ceramic, graphite, surlyn** These are all modern hi-tech materials used for putter heads and inserts. They can be designed in varying degrees of hardness and feel. They are usually expensive so protection is recommended.

● **Wooden** The original type of putter head dating back to the nineteenth-century mallet design. They have great feel but are inconsistent, so precision striking is necessary. These must be kept in putter covers.

● **Zinc alloy** Used in very cheap putters. Light and brittle, they can snap in the neck and do not have good balance or feel.

Putter head weight

The general rule of thumb is that the speed of the greens on which you play regularly should dictate the weight of

putter you use: light weight for fast greens, and heavier for slow greens.

There are, of course, exceptions, and the touring professional playing on different speed greens from week to week will not necessarily change putters each time, although some do.

It is a good idea to have a very heavy putter to use for practice. This will encourage a smooth unhurried stroke and avoids the feeling that the putter head will leave its correct swing line.

Above: The putter head can be made heavier by adding self-adhesive lead tape (available from most PGA pro shops). It is worth trying if you leave a lot of putts short of the hole.

Left: Here is a putter that has built in weight adjustment parts which can be filled with solid metal or cork spaces.

Choosing a putter

The goose neck or offset head

This is designed to encourage your hands to be positioned forward of the striking face, and the line drawn down the front of the putter shaft will dissect a part of the ball. Obviously the degree of offset can vary but it is a factor of which you should be aware.

Loft

You may think that putters have no loft but, in fact, a small amount of between two and four degrees is an essential ingredient. When a golf ball is putted, it produces a skidding action for the first 20 per cent of its movement, and then it rolls for the remaining 80 per cent.

If a putter had no loft, then the ball would be pinched into the ground and would then skip and bounce; you would have less directional and distance control – and hence the necessity for a small amount of loft.

Above: Three putter heads showing varying degrees of offset: (from the left) no offset; ¼ inch offset; ½ inch offset.

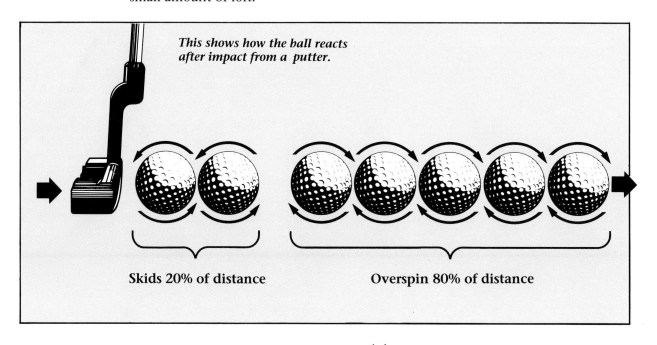

This shows how the ball reacts after impact from a putter.

Skids 20% of distance   Overspin 80% of distance

14

The shaft

Shaft options

Allied to the head weight is the shaft material; the lighter the shaft the more weight may be placed in the putter head. Most putter shafts will be steel with the light weight choices being aluminium, fibreglass and, more recently, graphite. You should also be aware of the flexibility of the shaft which can considerably change the overall feel of the putter. A more flexible shaft will give a very good feel on contact but is difficult to control for distance; a stiffer shaft is likely to be more consistent. The old fashioned wooden hickory shaft gave a very good feel but was inclined to move a lot more causing the face to open and close.

Some steel shaft putters have a bend near the head that lines the top part of the shaft with the centre of

Different shaft materials: (from left to right) graphite; black coated steel; wooden (Hickory); fibreglass (ladies); steel (chromed).

gravity of the putter head. This produces a face balanced effect which you can check by balancing the putter shaft on your finger – notice how the face is horizontal. Using this test with a straight shaft you will see the toe of the putter swing down towards the ground.

Some steel shafts have a stepped shaft like an iron club, but this can be considered as a visual interference, in which case a smoothly tapered shaft is preferable to the eye.

A centre shaft putter with the sweet spot marked. This model may be used left- or right-handed.

15

Choosing a putter

Shaft length

This is a choice made by preference but should also be influenced by your height and build. If the putter is too long for you it will prohibit you from standing correctly with your eyes over the ball; if it is too short you will have to crouch too much.

It is good to experiment with different length putters but remember that a short shaft will reduce the club head swingweight, and the longer the shaft, the heavier the putter head will feel.

Left: A flat lie angle requires you to stand further from the ball. Above: This upright lie allows the feet to be closer to the ball with the hands in a higher position.

Lie angle

The distance you wish to stand from the ball and position of your hands will require you to select a putter with the correct lie. The angle between the sole and the shaft is critical, and so the putter must rest flat on the ground with the grip in a comfortable position for your hands. A putter with a rounded sole from toe to heel does allow for a little variation in this, whereas a flat sole needs precise fitting. Otherwise, you risk snagging either the toe or heel of the putter into the ground. In both cases, the point on the sole directly below the sweet spot or centre of the face should be soled.

This putter has a very light graphite shaft (and lightweight leather grip), which, combined with its head weighting, defies gravity to stand on its own. It is particularly good for checking your aim by standing behind the line of putt.

Left: A close-up of two different lie angles; both putter soles are flat to the ground but notice the shaft angles.

Choosing a putter

The grip

Your only contact with the putter is, of course, through the handle, and your hands control the way the putter face returns to strike the ball so it is an important element. Comfort is the main consideration but look for a putter grip with a flat surface down the front as this will encourage your hands to square the club face each time.

The round-type grip used on woods and irons is not so good, but check that the flat spot on the putter grip has been aligned properly with the face. Unfortunately, often this is not the case with some putters.

The thickness of the grip is worth experimenting with, and there are now putters available with oversize grips, the theory being that the larger grip makes

Six different putter grips all featuring the preferable flat front surface to aid alignment of your hands. The top two are leather, the middle two are composite, and the bottom two are rubber.

# Putting

it easier to eliminate unwanted hand and wrist movement. If your directional control is not so good, you may find that this may help you.

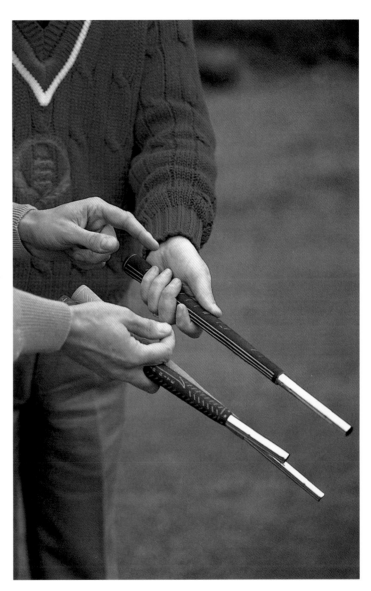

These pictures show the correct grip thickness fitting for a set of clubs. The same principle should be applied when fitting a putter grip – the fingers should just meet the fleshy part of the thumb joint (above right). Experimenting with a thinner grip (above) or a thicker grip (top) is acceptable when putting but must be precise for all other clubs.

Choosing a putter

The extra long shafted putter

Below: Note the squareness of the shoulders, how the eyes are over the ball and how the left-hand knuckles and first finger joints form a rectangle relating to the putter face.

Right: Stand fairly upright with a square alignment and stance. The right-hand position is a light touch between thumb and index finger to help you 'feel' the length of the putt. Above: Note the square putter head and square stance.

A recent innovation given recognition in Europe by Sam Torrance and widely used in the United States on the Senior Tour, these putters vary in length between 105cm/42in and 125cm/50in compared with the 89cm/35½in average putter shaft length.

If you have tried many methods and styles and still experience frustration with your putting, it is worth considering the very long shaft option. Many of its converts do honestly believe that it is a better method and not just a desperate last resort, although there is a slight stigma attached to having a putter protruding from the golf bag 15cm/6in higher than the longest wood.

The technique is totally different to that of a conventional shot and requires the hands to be split by as much as 45cm/18in with two gripping points. The left hand holds the top of the handle, with the index finger and thumb uppermost against either the chin or the centre of the chest. The right hand is then positioned on the lower handle with the shaft running through the 'V' formed between the thumb and the index finger in a similar fashion to a snooker bridge hand. The fingers should be outstretched so that the palm faces the target.

The top part of the shaft remains in one position and becomes the fulcrum of the swing movement although there is still some shoulder rocking as in the pendulum stroke.

The putter head must be designed specially because the lie angle is more upright than a standard putter, the shaft being very close to vertical and your feet positioned close to the ball.

This method can work very effectively but it is like learning to putt all over again and requires a fair amount of practice before you will be able to put your faith in it on the course.

Finding the sweet spot

How to find the sweet spot of a putter: hold the shaft lightly between thumb and forefinger, then tap the putter face using a pencil with a rubber on its end. At the point that the putter does not twist you establish its centre of gravity, or sweet spot.

Summary

I cannot stress enough the importance that you should place on your putting, especially as most amateur golfers neglect this department of the game. You should not be satisfied with the average two putts per hole, 36 putts per round. Try and reduce the total to around 30 or less – you can always improve.

It is good to experiment with different putters: try swapping putters with a friend for a short time, and look closely at the putters used by other players. You never know what you may be missing.

Most PGA professionals keep a large selection of putters in their shops because they recognise the value of good putting. Don't be afraid to seek your pro's advice and ask if you can try out some of the putters on the practice putting green before you commit yourself.

CHAPTER TWO

The putting grip

by David Johnson

Good preparation is the key to the consistent execution of any successful golf shot, and putting is no exception. Over the years, numerous golf instructors have written about and taught the correct putting grip, but most poor putters just do not bother to implement it. Unless you prepare for your putting stroke correctly, by perfecting a good and consistent relationship between your hands and the way you place them upon the handle of your putter, putting will always be a game of chance. We are going to try to remove the chance element from the putting game and produce the sort of relationship between you and your putter that a musician has whilst in tune with the rest of his orchestra.

This grip (left) is used by Bernhard Langer. After the problems he had with his putting, he adopted this grip to give him the confidence to putt well and to stay at the top of professional golf. The top of the shaft is held against the left forearm. It is virtually the same as the normal grip (as shown opposite) except that the left hand is reversed at the bottom of the shaft, with the right hand at the top of the shaft securing it against the left forearm. This helps to promote a smooth pendulum putting motion.

23

The putting grip

Choice of grips in holding the putter

There are numerous ways in which people hold the putter. Most players used to prefer the straightforward **over-lapping**, or **Vardon, grip** where all the fingers of the left hand were simply placed around the rubber handle, with the thumb lying on top of the handle and the back of the hand facing towards

The Vardon (overlapping) grip
The correct way to build the grip: lay the grip of the club across your left hand from a point at the first joint of the index finger through the palm into the butt of the hand. Close the fingers round the shaft with the thumb pointing down the centre of the shaft. Place the palm of the right hand facing the hole, the little finger of the right hand overlapping the index finger of the left hand. The thumb of the right hand will be pointing down the shaft.

the target. The ring finger of the right hand is placed against the index finger of the left hand whilst folding the remaining fingers of the right hand round the handle, resting the little finger in the recess between the index and second fingers of the left hand. The thumb of the right hand is placed upon the top of the handle, which ensures that the palm of the right hand is facing the target.

Golfers with small hands will find that when the little finger of the right hand overlaps the index finger of the left hand, it rests on top of the index finger. However, for people with long fingers, the little finger will rest in the cleft between the index finger and the third finger.

The putting grip

Another popular grip was the **interlocking grip** where the left hand takes the same position as with the Vardon grip, but, as the right hand closes round the handle, the little finger of the right hand interlocks with the index finger of the left hand, thereby interlocking the hands together, and hence the name, interlocking grip.

The interlocking grip
Build this grip in the same way as in the Vardon grip with the shaft resting across your left hand. Extend the left index finger and place the palm of the right hand facing the hole. Instead of overlapping the little finger over the left-hand index finger, interlock it between the index finger and third finger as shown in the photograph.

Note the difference as shown here between the interlocking and Vardon (overlapping) grips.

The putting grip

A third grip which was often favoured by golfers with very small hands or short fingers, particularly juniors and ladies, was the **two-handed, or baseball grip**. Again, the left hand is placed on the handle as in the Vardon grip. To complete the grip, place all four fingers of the right hand at the bottom side of the handle with fingers facing upwards; now apply similar pressure with all fingers whilst closing both fingers and palm around the handle. The right thumb is placed on top of the handle with the muscular base of the right thumb covering the left thumb.

The major problem that arises from using these orthodox grips is a tendency to encourage wrist action which is accepted when you are on form, but can lead to an inconsistent putting action. To help avoid such an action as over-active wrists, players have tried many variations on the old themes from placing the index finger of one or both hands down the handle of the putter, to overlapping with two fingers of the right hand onto the left hand.

Another method tried by many is the reverse grip, whereby in the case of a right-handed player, the hands are

The baseball grip
Build the grip in exactly the same way as before with the left hand. However, note that all the fingers and thumbs must be on the shaft and the hands must be close together.

reversed into a left-handed position, simply by placing the hands onto the handle as if you were going to play left handed, with the left hand beneath the right hand.

Most of the different variations have been tried to minimize wrist action. Players were beginning to imagine that to be able to putt well, you required the delicate touch of a surgeon together with his dexterity. However, the truth is that a good touch has to be learnt and achieved with practice. Consider today's top professionals with their tremendous ability to hit the ball incredible distances; this is not achieved by brute strength alone but by the improved modern method used. A golfer nowadays cannot be that much stronger than in previous generations.

The putting grip

The reverse overlap grip

The purpose of the putting grip is to reduce the influence of the wrists by placing the handle more in the palms of both hands, thus creating a more passive grip allowing the shoulder to initiate the pendulum action of the stroke.

To achieve the desired grip, place the club handle diagonally across the heel pad of the left hand; you should find that by laying the club across the pads you take the fingers off it to a great extent. The tips of the fingers only should be on the grip; your left index finger is off the club completely extending downwards and lying on the fingers of the right hand with your left thumb placed on the top of the handle running straight down. In the right hand, the handle rests at the base of the index finger, the ring finger of the right hand lying snugly against the middle finger of the left hand.

 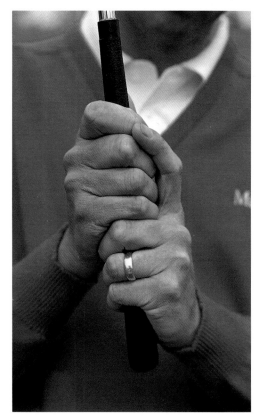

The reverse overlap grip
Start building the grip with the left hand as before with the left hand little finger

extended. The right-hand grip should also be as before but without overlapping or interlocking. All the fingers of the right

30

The handle runs diagonally up across the palm towards a spot just under the heel pad. It is important that the club does not actually rest in the right palm. The fleshy part of your hand just under that heel pad should rest against the middle finger of your left hand. Your right thumb should be just to the left side of the handle so that it cannot exert any pressure and influence the putting stroke.

In contrast to the grip that you use for full golf shots, the right palm does not face the left palm. In fact, the right hand is turned slightly clockwise or under just a few degrees – this should keep the hand in a relaxed position. This grip is called the reverse overlap grip.

Please remember that practice makes perfect. The more time and trouble you take to perfect the relation-ship your hands have with the putter the better your chances of perfecting the action. Next time you are out on the practice green, try this grip out for your-self and see the improvement.

hand take up their natural position on the grip but the index finger of the left hand will overlap the first three fingers of the right hand.

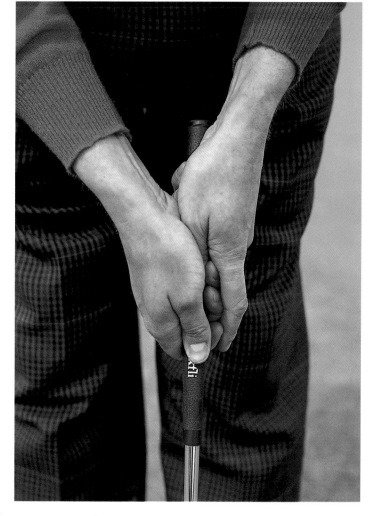

The putting grip

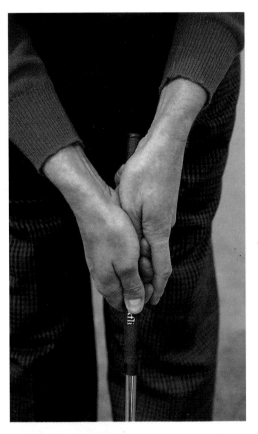

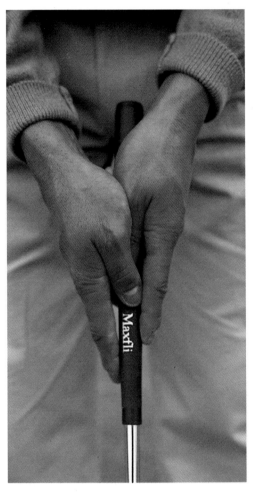

The two-finger reverse overlap grip

In this variation of the normal reverse overlap grip, both index fingers of the right and left hands are pointing straight down the shaft instead of overlapping or interlocking. Note that the fingers must be straight down the shaft and opposing each other. Be careful not to move the fingers slightly across the shaft as shown.

The split hands grip

This is a most dangerous grip although it is used successfully by some golfers. The angles across the back of the left hand and the palm of the right hand must be correct as in all other grips, i.e. parallel to one another, or the hands will work against each other. This should not be advocated as a good solid grip, and it is definitely not suitable for beginners.

The side-saddle stance grip

This technique is the croquet-type way of putting. Again, although some golfers have found it to be successful if they have experienced problems with their putting, most professionals would not recommend it and it is seldom used by good putters.

CHAPTER THREE

The set up
and stroke

by Alasdair Barr

When it comes to style in the putting stance it is fair to say that literally anything goes. Comfort is the basic requirement and only the individual player will know how that feels. You only have to look at a handful of the top tournament professionals to see all the different stances and most of those were arrived at by trial and error. In fact, it is not uncommon for a tournament player to alter his stance during a tournament round if the one he is using is not proving successful.

Seve Ballesteros has a fairly narrow stance and is quite crouched over the ball. On the other hand, Nick Faldo, a tall man, has a wide stance and a short putter and this sets him quite low over the ball, and no one putted better in 1990 than him. Ben Crenshaw, the 1984 US Masters Champion has a very upright stance and stands well away from the ball. He has probably been the most successful putter over a long period of time. As you can see, it is very much a case of try it and see. However, to get you started in this most frustrating part of the game I will give you some recommendations and guidelines.

The set up and stroke

The set up

The set up or starting position requires you to follow a certain sequence to help establish consistency. As with all golf shots from the full-blooded tee shot to the short putt, the set up goes a long way to controlling the swinging movement, so we will examine each stage of that set up. As many a good PGA teaching professional will tell you, a good set up will not guarantee a good shot but a bad set up will guarantee a bad one.

It is absolutely vital in the putting stroke that your body remains steady as any movement will affect the angle of the putter head. The set up goes a long way to help achieve this, and do remember that comfort is the key.

The set up sequence

Now let us look at the sequence we have to follow. You have already learned how to hold the putter, so now you need to position your body.

1 Aim
2 Stance and posture
3 Ball position
4 Stroke

To help you keep things simple, start with a putt that is straight.

Aim The putter head must be set with its front edge at right angles to the intended target – we shall call this the *ball-to-target line*. This is important as the putter head needs to be held at this angle throughout the complete stroke. No matter how good the stroke, the wrong aim will destroy everything.

The shoulders, too, should be

parallel to this line as the hands and arms can only work along the line of the shoulders. I strongly suggest this square stance as a starting position but, as I stated earlier, you always make your own adjustments as you gain in experience. Always remember the old adage that 'if it works, it's right'.

Stance and posture On the shortish putts of, say, up to 10 feet, the feet should be positioned about 12 inches apart. An imaginary line drawn through the toes of the shoes should run parallel to the ball-to-target line.

This is called a square stance and will encourage the club and body to work together.

The weight should be positioned slightly on the right leg which will give you the feeling of staying 'behind' the ball and being able to stroke the ball more towards the hole. The knees should be slightly flexed and the weight distributed between the balls of the feet and the heels. The arms should hang comfortably from the shoulders with

your elbows close to your body. This position will help the putter and your hands and arms work as a unit and stop the putter waving about during the stroke.

Bend over from the hips so that your eyes are over the ball. How much you should bend from the hips is determined by how far you stand from the ball. Again, comfort is the deciding factor provided that it keeps you in good balance. To help position the eyes correctly over the ball take up the position I have just described and hold another ball level with your eyes. Then drop the ball and it will land on the ball on the putting green.

Ball position The ball can be played

Opposite top: This set up is wrong. The bottom leading edge of the putter is not 90 degrees to the player's stance. The blade is open to the target, sending the ball to the right of it. Opposite: This set up is correct. The bottom leading edge of the blade is square to the target and stance. Left: The weight is slightly back on the right side and the hands are slightly behind the putter head. This enables you to strike the ball slightly on the upswing to make it roll. However, you can distribute your weight evenly or even favour the left leg as is taught by many PGA pros. Doing this can cause you to hit the ball slightly on the downswing and I would not personally recommend it. In fact, many of the world's top golfing stars always favour the right leg, and I would advocate this method.

The set up and stroke

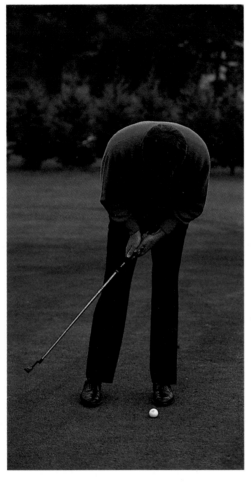

Above: These movements have been accentuated but the sequence shows how too much weight on the left side can cause an incorrect angle of attack and the

collapse of the arm position. The player has lost his address position and is fighting the movement of the swing to get the blade through to the target.

anywhere between the left heel and the centre of the feet. This will create a very slight upward hit on the ball imparting overspin, which helps to make the ball roll better end over end across the green. You do not have to try to make this happen as it is automatic. When you swing the putter head it is at its lowest point at the centre of the stance. Prior to that it is on the downswing, and after that it is on the upswing, so you can see

that the desired effect is created by the ball position. If the ball were to be placed further back than centre the descending blow would cause the ball to jump or hop into the air and loss of control would occur. The hands should be held level or slightly ahead of the ball in the set up as this makes it easier to keep the wrists firm and allows the hands to lead the club head through the stroke.

The stroke The basic concept of the putting stroke is to create a pendulum-like effect. The putter is swung with the hands and arms at an even pace. Within that stroke the length of the backswing controls the distance, and the follow through controls the direction. In that respect it can be likened to throwing a ball underarm. Just try throwing a ball and take a look at yourself as you perform the movement. Swing your arm back and through at an even pace and notice how far the ball travels. Now attempt to make the ball go further and you will notice that it is the length of the backswing that has increased. Adding greater leverage allows you to make the ball travel a greater distance.

Now on that initial throw did you stop moving your hand the minute you let the ball go? I very much doubt it. By following through you were actually indicating to the ball where you wanted it to go, i.e. *direction*.

Backswing = distance

Throughswing = direction

On your underarm throw, notice that there is not any movement at the wrist – putting is identical to this. Wrist action makes it very difficult to control the putter head angle throughout the stroke.

Now to achieve this within your pendulum stroke you must try to make the length of the backswing and forward swing at worst equidistant. However, it will not do any harm if the forward swing is fractionally longer. You can actually follow through as far as you wish and it will have no bearing on the distance provided that the club is swung at an even pace. However, if you do not do this, you will seriously affect the distance as the putter head will be decelerating into the ball and this creates a quitting effect and the putt will finish short of the target. As Lee Trevino said, "Putts that finish short of the hole have no chance of going in!"

The sweet spot

The ball has to be positioned in line with what is referred to as the 'sweet spot' on the putter blade – if you strike the ball anywhere else on the head it can cause mishits and clearly this will cause the ball to miss the target. The sweet spot can be found by holding the putter aloft with two fingers at the grip end and tapping the putter face with the forefinger. When you tap the putter face and it swings without deviating or twisting, you have found the sweet spot and this is where the ball must be struck. If you have any trouble or are uncertain about this, your local PGA professional will advise you. A lot of putters these days have a guide line on top of the head but check it anyway with the above method.

Practice drill

To practise this effect I would suggest that either on the carpet at home or on a practice putting green, you place two tee pegs an equal distance on either side of the golf ball and just swing the putter

The set up and stroke

back and through to each tee peg. You will then achieve the feeling of the pendulum type of effect and also just how far the ball will travel from this basic stroke. Once this has been performed on about six balls you will then be able to vary the length of the stroke to vary the distance.

As you can see from the practice drill, you actually stroke a putt as opposed to hitting it. The strike on the ball comes from the stroke and the ball is made contact with because it is in the way of the putter head. Most putts are missed because the length of the backswing is too short and the putter head has to be forced through with the wrists thereby causing a change of speed and affecting the angle of the club head. Regardless of the length of the putt, the path along which the putter is swung is straight back and through, and the easiest way to help you achieve this is to try and keep the putter head as close to the ground as you can manage, particu-

Below: This sequence shows the complete putting stroke – the set up, take back and follow through back to the original starting address position. This is a useful practice drill using the tee pegs as your ball-to-target line. Note that the distances taken back and followed through are the same.

larly on the backswing.

The benefits of a straight path are clear if you consider the alternatives. It is absolutely essential that the whole body must remain steady throughout the stroke. As I advised you earlier, it is totally a hand-and-arm stroke. To encourage your body to remain still, the head must be held in position until such time as the follow through has been completed. If your head was to follow the ball, then the shoulders would turn to point left of the target, and as the hands and arms work along this line the putter head would close (i.e. aim to the left of the hole). After the putt has been stroked successfully the putter head at the follow through should be able to return to its starting position. Another useful aid to keep the body steady is to exhale slightly just prior to starting the stroke.

Putts fall into two distinct categories: the ones you are trying to hole; and the long distance putts which,

40

although it would be nice to hole out, you are really only trying to get close enough to make the next putt a formality, so as to avoid the greatest sin in golf – three putting or worse!

On the holeable variety, you follow all the guidelines we have laid down. However, on the longer putts when we need to lengthen the pendulum stroke the distance needs to be increased between the feet. The longer the putt, the wider the stance. I would suggest that you start off by considering the putts of 8 to 10 feet as the holeable ones.

The forward press

If you experience any great difficulty in getting the putting stroke started on a smooth basis you can incorporate what is called the 'forward press'. This is a slight forward movement of the hands towards the hole. This will then cause a very slight recoil, and the movement can help initiate the backswing smoothly. Rhythm is all important as a nice smooth stroke encourages consistency. A light grip will help also.

Summary

Your aim and alignment of the putter head are vitally important as it is impossible to be consistently successful if these are wrong. Remember, too, that your eyes must be over the ball-to-target line and the head held level and not twisted to the right or left, as this will adversely affect the stroke. The eyes will be slightly behind the ball and this is achieved by the weight distribution favouring the right leg (only slightly, remember). This makes it marginally easier to see the line of the putt from the set-up position. When you sight the putt from the set-up position do so by rotating your eyes up and down the line, and not by lifting the head as this destroys the set up that you have worked so hard to achieve; it is not always easy to return to the original position.

Remember on the tee shots that the target is approximately 50 yards wide. The greens for the approach shots are roughly 25 yards wide, but for putting the hole is less than five inches wide. As you can see, such a target leaves you no room for error.

Practice is vital to improve any part of your golf game but particularly so in putting. As putting accounts for roughly half of the strokes used in playing the game, the top professionals devote at least half of their practice time to the putting green. It is impossible to score well if your putting is suspect.

A bad player can score if he can putt – a good player will struggle, no matter how well he strikes the ball if he can't finish on the greens. So follow the 'rules' that I have laid down – plenty of practice and, hopefully, this will lead to success on the greens.

CHAPTER FOUR

The pendulum putting swing

by Nigel Blenkarne

We have already established that the object of a efficient putting stroke is to roll the ball across the green on the correct line and at the correct speed for each given distance. To achieve these aims you need to keep the ball rolling on the putting surface and not jumping up into the air; if the ball does leave the ground it will almost certainly pull up short of the hole and can also jump off line. Sometimes the quality of the green is responsible for an irregular roll, but it is commonplace for the golfer to blame the green when really it is the player's putting action that is causing the problem.

For a consistent feel for distance and line you must strike the ball with the sole of your putter remaining horizontal – parallel to the ground as you contact the ball. You must avoid hitting the ball on either a downward or upward approach, both of which will cause the ball to hop and not produce the desired rolling action.

In recent years the majority of good golfers have adopted the *pendulum-type* stroke because they find it easier to obtain a level contact this way.

The putter is kept level with the ball's equator for at least nine inches either side of the ball, which is positioned just inside the left heel. The backswing and forward swing are equal in length.

The pendulum putting swing

Angle of the club head

The putter should meet the ball with its sole parallel to the ground.

The putter is hitting down on the ball too much, and the hands are too far in front of the putter face.

The ball is being struck too much on the upswing, and the hands are too far behind the putter head.

The result of a bad angle

This sequence shows that either a downward or upward contact on the ball will result in an uneven roll giving poor distance and direction control.

The pendulum putting swing

Crown green bowls may be compared to putting, the bowler's hand releasing the bowl as it travels low to the ground. It is neither dropped down nor thrown up. You can also consider how smooth the bowling action is – a rolling movement, not a throwing one. Try to reproduce these ideas in your putting stroke.

A bowls action where the ball is released from the hand low to the ground to produce a rolling movement which is similar to a good putting stroke.

The set up

You should adopt a posture with more bend forwards from your hips than your normal golf set up. If you drop a vertical line down from the front of your shoulders it will fall a few inches in front of your toe line, but do not put all your weight on your toes. As with other golf shots, your weight should be distributed evenly between the balls of your feet and the heels.

Your arms do not need to be straight for putting, so let each elbow point inwards towards the corresponding hip bone and with your elbows held inwards towards each other. Avoid having your arms pressed hard against your body because this will prohibit you from keeping your body still while your arms move.

Although it is not essential, it is

Right: A good putting set up. The eyes are over the ball, the hands are away from legs and the elbows are pointing inwards towards the hips. Above: The comparison to the distance you would stand from the ball when hitting a full shot. Notice the shaft angles in both photographs.

The pendulum putting swing

The putter grip should fall more into the left palm than it does for other shots (right). Notice the curve formed by the wrist.

preferable to hold your hands in a high position; this gives the wrists a better chance to remain firm throughout your stroke. You should notice now that the putter shaft is much nearer a vertical line (but not quite vertical) than it is for a normal golf shot and therefore you will be standing a lot closer to the ball. You will also be aware that the putter grip falls more into the palm of your left hand than for full shots.

Above left: The hands are held high – the correct position for a pendulum stroke.
Above: The hands are too close to the body; this will produce a wristy action.

The pendulum putting swing

Grip

Quite a number of grip variations may be used successfully for putting, the most popular of which (and the one recommended for the pendulum strike) is the reverse overlap grip as described in Chapter Two.

The length of the putter you use must also be considered and is an important factor to get right. If your putter shaft is too long it will cause you to stand up too straight with your arms too bent; if it is too short, you will crouch over too much and your arms will be too straight. However, some excellent pendulum putters have used a very short shaft and kept both arms absolutely straight, notably Andy North, twice US Open winner.

Above: A putter shaft that is too short produces a crouched posture.

Above: A long putter shaft will cause too upright a posture; note that the eye line is not over the ball.

Body alignment

Your feet and shoulder alignment should be parallel with the ball-to-hole line (for a straight putt). Picture a rect- angle whereby the point at which your feet are aimed is equidistant from the hole as your feet are from the ball.

Left: Your feet, knees, hips and shoulders should all point parallel to your target line. The ball to the right of the hole is the same distance from the hole as the player stands from the object ball.

Above: Always imagine that the ball is rolling hard enough to go just past the hole.

The pendulum putting swing

The ball is positioned too far back in the stance causing the hands to be in front of the putter head, creating a downward contact.

Ball position

The ball position in your stance may be experimented with, but the recommendation would be from just inside the left heel. It should not move back further than the centre. The object is to contact the ball on a level approach, not upwards or downwards.

Unlike any other shot your eye line should be directly over the ball. The easiest method of checking this is to adopt your set-up position and then take a second ball and hold it between your eyes, on the bridge of your nose. Simply let it fall and it should land on top of the ball you are playing.

Right: This ball position would be correct if the player moved his hands forward (far right). This would produce an upward contact.

Putting

Above: Adopting a normal putting set up – hold a ball with the right hand on the bridge of your nose. Above right: When the ball is dropped, it should hit the ball on the ground. This checks that your eye line is over the ball.

Pre-stroke drills

It is not a good idea to stand absolutely motionless for too long before you putt. Here are some good thoughts to avoid freezing over the ball:

● Tap the ground very lightly just behind the ball before you start your stroke.

● Do not push down into the ground by resting your weight on the putter.

● Make small movements with your feet to get really settled.

● Press your hands forward, towards the target, just prior to the takeaway.

Body weight

Finally, your weight should be distributed slightly in favour of your left leg, approximately 60:40.

As in all golf shots, the set up is of paramount importance for the putting stroke. You cannot hope to make a good putt from a bad address position.

The pendulum putting swing

The pendulum

Having established a sound aim and address you can now focus your thoughts on producing the pendulum movement.

This method is designed to reduce your hand and wrist action to a minimum with no breaking or hinging of your left wrist on the forward swing. It is normally excessive wrist break and over-active hands that result in inconsistent ball contact and poor control of distance. Using the pendulum, you

Above: The address position. Right: The left shoulder has moved down, right shoulder up from the set up. The putter grip, shaft and head move at the same pace. Note that the impact position is identical to the address. The triangle and shaft relationship is maintained. The head, body and legs have remained still.

should promote the feeling of a stroke as opposed to a hit, with the putter travelling at a constant speed throughout, not decelerating nor accelerating much either. The distance the ball travels is then governed by the length of your stroke.

The fundamental object is to form a triangle made up of your arms and shoulders, which then moves from a fulcrum at the back and base of your neck. Concentrate on keeping your legs, body and head very steady and feel your shoulders rocking back and forth.

This movement is not the same as the full golf swing which requires the shoulders to turn around the trunk. During the putting stroke you should

The pendulum putting swing

feel that on the backswing your right shoulder moves up slightly whereas your left moves down slightly. On the follow through the reverse takes place – the left shoulder moves up and the right moves down.

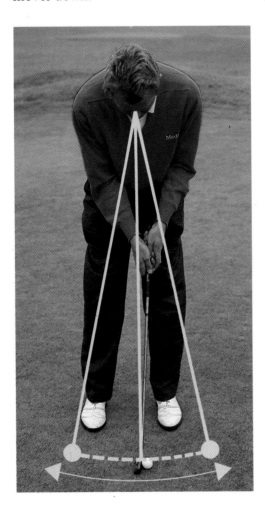

Consistent pace to gauge distance

The two major factors in making a good putt are direction and distance. Let us focus on the distance element first because it is often the misjudgement of speed, especially on middle- and long-range putts, which leads to poor putting results. Consider for a moment how often you have been six feet short or six feet long on a putt; whereas even on a very badly directed line you are unlikely to be more than two or three feet off line. On very fast and sloping greens, of course, the line and pace go hand in hand and influence each other a lot more.

The pendulum putting stroke is generally considered more reliable in producing a better feel for distance than a harsh hitting action. As its name suggests, the backswing and follow through should correspond in length, like the movement of a clock pendulum.

So often a golfer will use the same length of stroke to hit the ball 10, 30 or even 50 feet and then attempt to hit it harder or softer. This, in turn, brings too much hand action into the stroke, so pay attention to ensure that the backswing is long enough to allow gradual acceleration without the need to add a speed rush with your hands. Adopt an attitude whereby the presence of the ball is almost incidental. It just happens to be in the way of the putter head as it moves smoothly through the middle part of the stroke. There should be no conscious hit at the ball.

Practice drill

In order to develop this concept it is far better to practise your stroke without aiming at a target. Take 6 balls on to a putting green and make strokes of varying length; two balls with a six-inch backswing and through swing, then two with a 12-inch swing, and two with an 18-inch movement back and forth, and so on. Keep your pace constant, concentrating on a consistent strike, and notice how the roll distance varies according to the stroke length. For a guide, place a tee in the ground 12 inches behind the ball and another tee 12 inches after the ball, this being placed an inch or so outside your intended target line. This exercise will give you an easy-to-check visual guide to the length of your stroke either side of the ball.

Tees are placed 12 inches on either side of the ball to help develop a backswing and follow through of equal length.

Once you have started to consistently develop a pendulum stroke action then introduce targets at varying distances and learn to feel how long the stroke must be to roll the ball your given measurement. Obviously, the speed of the green must be accounted for; a 10-foot putt on a slow green will require a *longer* stroke than a 10-foot putt on a fast green.

The pendulum putting swing

Direction

The ball's travel is influenced by:

1 Your aim.

2 The face of your putter at impact.

3 The swing line that the putter head moves along either side of the ball.

The putting stroke is a mini version of a full golf swing, the one major difference being that you stand much closer to the ball than for any full shot. It thus follows that the arc that the putter head moves on is far less pronounced. The middle section, nine inches either side of the ball should be straight, so for your short putts there is no curve in the swing. It is only for longer putts that the pendulum starts to include a slight curve inside on both the backswing and follow through.

The tees indicate an incorrect stroke line which is too curved; the putter head should follow the white line for at least nine inches on either side of the ball.

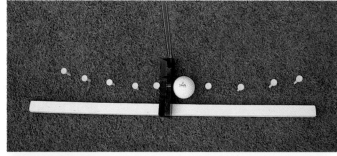

The tees show an incorrect out-to-in stroke line.

The tees show an incorrect in-to-out stroke line.

The putter face must return at impact at 90 degrees to the stroke line (far left). An incorrect open face (centre), an incorrect closed face (left).

One benefit of your pendulum stroke is that because the wrists are locked there will be minimal rotation of your forearms and wrists, and therefore the striking surface of your putter will remain at 90 degrees to the putter head's travel. On a long putt there will be a small degree of opening the putter face on the backswing and closing it on the forward swing, but this should not be a conscious thought – certainly not on short and middle range putts.

Provided that you move the putter on a straight line through the ball and there is no manipulation of your hands, you will be producing accurate and consistent direction.

One final aspect of the pendulum must be mentioned, and that is the curve of the arc of the putter head in relation to the ground.

The fulcrum being at the back of your neck likens it to that point at the centre of a circle or wheel, while your arms and putter shaft are the radius. Your fulcrum must not change position, and therefore the longer your stroke, the further from the ground the putter will finish. Again, the centre section must be close to the ground to achieve a level contact on the ball, but beyond the nine inches on either side of the ball the putter head must rise gradually.

Recap the key thoughts

- The putter face must aim at your target (the hole for a straight putt).
- Your feet and body line should aim slightly left.
- Your shoulders, arms, hands and putter shaft move together, as one unit.
- Your legs, body and head remain still.
- The backswing and forward swing should be equal in length.
- Keep the pace of the stroke constant.

The pendulum putting swing

This sequence for a long putt shows how a slight arc develops beyond the straight centre section of the stroke. This can be seen from the overhead photographs.

Above: From the ground view, this sequence shows that the putter head must be allowed to rise gradually as it swings back and through. This is not a conscious lifting from the ground but an integral part of the pendulum.

The pendulum putting swing

Variations and practice drills

The cross-hand method
(left hand below right)

This technique has been used successfully by a number of professionals on the Tour, notably Bernhard Langer and Bruce Leitzke. Having the left hand lower on the grip gives the feeling that the wrist will not hinge and that both hands keep moving towards the target more easily. The pendulum ideas are very much encouraged but this method is better employed only on short and medium-range putts. It may be too radical to use on the course but try it on the practice green occasionally.

Langer has adapted the method still further by holding his left hand well down the shaft and then clamping the top of the putter handle against the inside of his left forearm with his right palm, which faces the target.

The cross-handed method gives the back of the left hand and wrist a firm feel, which reduces any independent hand action.

Above right and right: The right hand is holding the putter grip firmly against the inside of the left forearm to further reduce hand action. Above: The same pendulum principles apply.

The pendulum putting swing

The cuff drill

You need to wear a jumper with a tight wrist cuff. Slide the top of the putter shaft inside your left sleeve and then take your normal putting grip with your right hand just onto the chrome of the shaft. Be aware of the putter grip staying against the inside of your left forearm throughout your stroke.

Note: This is not permitted during a round.

Above: Slide the putter handle inside the cuff of a tight jumper and grip lower down the club. Right: Keeping the end of the *putter grip against the inside of the left forearm is a practice routine to help promote the pendulum feeling.*

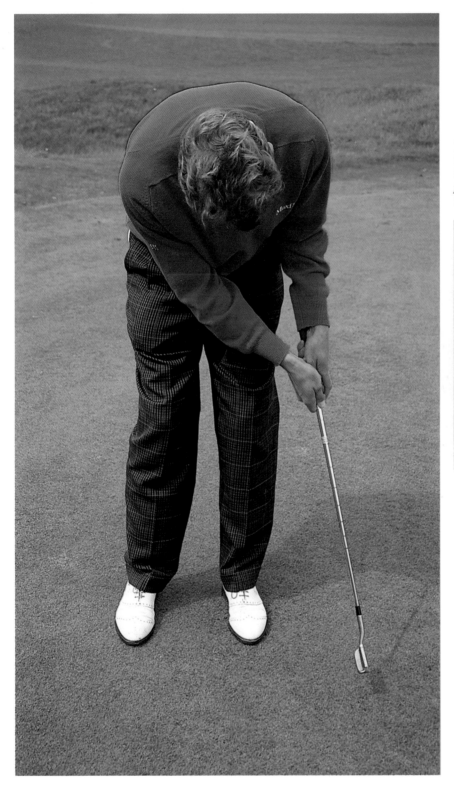

This position must be avoided; the left wrist has hinged so that the back of the hand points skywards instead of towards the hole.

The putting grip

The long-shafted practice putter

Some professionals have an adapted practice putter which has a shaft 12 to 15 inches longer than standard. The grip is held at normal length so the shaft extension rests along the inside of the left forearm to a point above the elbow. This will, of course, promote the feeling of a key thought – the arms and putter shaft moving together.

Conclusion

The putting element of golf is often neglected and dismissed as being a separate game. How often do you hear "I played great, but I couldn't putt"? You cannot be judged to have played well unless you putt well, especially as, on average, putting consumes 43 per cent of the strokes for the better player.

When most golfers start playing, putting is relatively easy and all efforts are focused on learning to hit full shots, but as the long game improves, putting plays a more important role in your score.

Many hundreds of thousands of golf lessons are given every year but how many of them are on putting? Very few professionals are ever asked to give a lesson on putting but it is in this vital part of the game that you can show most improvement quite quickly, and that will be reflected instantly in lower scoring and greater enjoyment. So spend as much time as you can practising your putting.

CHAPTER FIVE

Judging distance and lining up putts

by Nick Allen

Putting has been called the game within a game and contains in itself many skill aspects that, if developed through practice, will lead to your all-round improvement on the greens. In addition to developing your putting stroke, you also need to acquire an understanding of many other factors that will affect your success on the greens. Develop your awareness of these by practising the exercises and evaluation techniques outlined in the following pages; they form a series of pre-shot considerations that should be built into your own systematic routine.

Even with a sound putting stroke you will not hole putts consistently unless you correlate your skill with an awareness of many other factors. Develop your stroke with these routines, and your understanding of how the variable elements can affect the art of putting will result in an improvement that will exceed your expectations.

Judging distance and lining up putts

Judging distance

Many experienced putters judge distance by feel alone; yet what exactly does this mean? In essence, it means that a player has the ability to look at the length of a putt, transmit that vision through to his senses, and gauge the speed and length of the stroke required.

Yet how is this skill achieved? In some cases it is through natural ability, but the majority of golfers will only reach this by having first developed a fundamental understanding which they then practise using the routines outlined here. Whether short, medium or long range, when you survey the length of a putt it is important that you develop the ability to estimate the length in specific terms, clearly making a statement of the length in your own mind.

Memorize your judgement of the length

The routine I want you to practise here is a process that eventually will lead you to judge distance accurately. On the course I want you to be able to judge instinctively whether a putt is three, six 10 or 26 feet..

Practice routine 1

On a practice putting green, select a flat area and accurately measure distances from the hole at three, six and nine feet. Mark these points with a tee peg and place four balls at each marker.

I believe it is vital to utilize the practice stroke which is a key to judging distance accurately. The weight and length of stroke that you feel during the simulating stage acts as a catalyst and assists you to repeat the performance with the ball. Practise this exercise for 20 to 30 minutes. While trying to hole the putts will be a natural goal, the main objective of this exercise is to focus intently on the speed and strength of the stroke required to roll the ball level with the hole.

Ensure that you go through the same routine and spend the same amount of time on each putt. This is important so that you can concentrate on the strength of your stroke before each putt and learn from analysing the feedback afterwards. Proceed with the first putt from three feet and monitor the strength of your stroke and where the ball finishes. Remember

Continued on page 72

70

Putting

The objective of this exercise is to 'feel' the pace required to roll the ball level or just past the hole. Allow your practice strokes to simulate the weight and length of stroke required at the ball. Putt from three to six to nine feet and then back to three feet. Then increase the distances, eg. to six, twelve and eighteen feet.

Judging distance and lining up putts

Practice routine 1 *Continued*

that it is not a priority of the routine that you hole every putt, if the ball reaches the hole but narrowly misses on either side, or travels beyond the hole but within six to eight inches, you will be performing the routine correctly. Proceed by graduating through the range of distances until you sense the feel required to gauge the length of putt. As you complete the final putt from each of the specified distances be particularly aware of the next putt and the increasing speed and strength that your stroke requires. By using fewer balls before increasing the distance, your ability to quickly adjust the strength of your putting stroke will be tested.

Practice routine 2

Now increase the distance by increments of six feet. Place the markers at six, 12 and 18 feet, and then further at 12, 24 and 36 feet. Practise at increasing and then at decreasing distances, i.e. at the short range proceed from three to six to nine feet, and then back from nine to three feet. To repeat: by continually varying the range in this way and using four balls from each marker, your awareness of length and judgement will be broadly tested. Remember that your key in this practice routine is to constantly retain in your memory the specific length of putt you are practising. As you progress through the principles of this chapter and some of the routines, you will realise that a key element running throughout is an ability to visualize images in your mind. Later I will give you some advice on how to sharpen your senses in this area. Finally, by committing the length of putt to memory and by taking practice strokes, your touch, feel and judgement ability will merge with the actual stroke.

Practice routine 3

The visual technique for measuring distance

When playing the course, use this visual technique for measuring distance.

1 Standing over the ball looking directly down at the line of a three-foot putt, focus your vision to graduate along a straight line from the ball and stop at the 12 inches point.

2 Continue allowing your eyeline

to follow to the two-foot point and then continue to the hole.

Continued on page 74

Above: On a long putt, you may find it beneficial to judge it from a sideways angle. Stand over the ball looking down at the line of a three-foot putt. Focus your vision to graduate along the line as outlined in the exercise.

Judging distance and lining up putts

Practice routine 3 *Continued*

You judge the length of any putt by visualizing the length in increments in this way. If I have a 10 foot-putt, through this visual process I 'see' three separate three-foot increments and the final 12 inches to the hole. For long putts, I establish the first 10 feet in this way and then visualize the distance at increasing increments of 10 feet all the way to the hole. It is important that you graduate your visualization in this way. My

Below: For longer putts, visualize three-foot increments to 10 feet, and then use 10-foot increments for the very long putts.

three-foot increments to 10 feet, and 10-foot increments upwards.

I suggest that you try this method first. The key is to use length increments for which you can create clear images, and obviously my suggestion can be adapted accordingly to the lengths of your choice.

I suggest that you use the foregoing routine for putts of up to 30 feet. It becomes difficult to visualize distance standing at the ball for excessively long putts, and you adapt the routine in this case by first marking your ball and carefully walking to the hole giving yourself a side view of the putt approximately 10 feet wide of the line between the ball and the hole.

Your ability to visualize beyond approximately 30 feet from behind the ball will be affected, whereas the side-view walk will enable you to graduate the increments in the manner shown to establish distance for the very long putts.

In summary, the ability to judge distance is achieved through a system of routines that are designed to improve your ability in visualizing and picturing distance mentally.

This will prove a vital link to the putting stroke you are developing.

system therefore works on the following basis:

I visualize firstly 12-inch increments to three feet, and then

Factors affecting speed and break

It is important at this stage to define two terms that form vital considerations on the putting green. The term **borrow** refers to the margin of distance the ball should be played either left or right of the hole (allowing for natural contours), which will account for the

Break

When you have decided on a line for a specific putt, once you have initiated the roll on that specific line, the extent to which the ball leaves that line is called the **break**.

In simple terms, for a putt that you might consider has a 12-inch break from left to right, i.e. as you look towards the hole the left side is higher than the

Left: The balls indicate a straight putt to the flag on a slope but the effect of the slope is shown at the third ball where the break of the slope starts to take effect and the ball ends up right of the target. Therefore if the ball finishes one foot right of the hole, the borrow is one foot left.

Left: The tee peg to the left of the third ball shows the correct line to the hole.

Judging distance and lining up putts

right, you might consider aiming 12 inches left of the hole 'borrowing' to allow for the curvature of the rolling ball.

Many factors that affect the speed and break of a putt change continually as you will learn. An appealing aspect of golf is the continual changes in the environment and the conditions in which we play the game. Putting has its own infinite and variable conditions with which you will learn to contend. it is possible on the golf course that a certain number of, or indeed all 18, greens may vary, and your evaluation and skill must be adapted accordingly.

Opposite and above: By aiming the ball to the left of the hole and moving in to the hole, you can get your line, and the break has been accounted for.

Weather

Over the course of a year you will notice that as the seasons change, the conditions and your approach to putting also changes. The more you can learn from this the better you will adapt. Yet changes in conditions are not as predictable as the changing seasons. Within successive days conditions may change, and quite often within the same day over the period of just four hours.

It is important that you understand in basic terms how the greens react to different weather conditions. Furthermore it is equally important to understand how greenkeeping practices throughout the year affect the playing characteristics of the greens.

Rain

Rainfall will slow the speed of the putting surface considerably. The underlying soil structure and its ability to drain water will affect the recovery time before regaining its original pace. You will find that inland greens on a clay base will recover their original speed slower than greens at seaside links courses, which, consisting of a sand-based structure, will recover faster after rainfall. In normal weather conditions you may find that every green on the course has similar playing characteristics. However, this can change after rainfall, especially if the specification varied during construction, Greens that are banked steeply or located in hollows will usually attract water from these levels, and excessive undulations on a green's surface will affect its ability to recover from rain. High and low levels

Judging distance and lining up putts

Seaside greens are usually much faster than inland ones, and the velocity of the wind dictates the line you take on a putt. The greens are sand-blown and therefore much harder and faster.

on the green will recover differently, and therefore putting characteristics within the same green can vary.

Natural drainage has to take place before a drying process can begin, although strong winds and warm temperatures will accelerate this process after rain. You must be aware of the practice of automatic watering during the day, and when dew exists during early morning. All these sources of water will slow down putting speed and reduce the break on the greens.

Sun

Under the continual pressure of high temperatures, the soil structure will harden, and as the grass cover dries the pace of the surface becomes faster. In extreme conditions you will find that

this becomes similar to putting in frost conditions where luck plays a major part.

Frost

Playing in these conditions virtually removes the skill in putting, but it is important that you are aware of the changing process that occurs as temperatures rise. While judgement regarding speed and break requires luck in these conditions, during heavy frost when the ground is compacted you can allow for a quicker speed and greater break. Conversely, as temperatures rise the rolling ball will start to gather ice and water, which will clearly slow down speed and reduce break considerably. In either event, putting in these conditions becomes a lottery.

Height of cut on the greens

The greenkeeper's objective is to produce the finest putting surface possible given the elements of weather that often affect this objective. The height of cut is the position at which the blades are set to mow the greens and this will have a distinct effect on your feel and judgement. In general, a greater height of cut will be employed in the spring and autumn, which will clearly slow putting speed and break on the greens. Conversely, during the busier part of the golfing year between summer and autumn, the height of cut will be lowered, producing faster surfaces and the need to allow for greater break. During the winter months when the grass is dormant, it can thin out and, depending on the temperature, the putting speed can vary. If the greens are not rested during the winter and the weather attracts busy periods, the greens can become compacted and fast to putt.

Hole position

According to the type of golf to be played on a given day, i.e. informal daily play, member competitions or even professional events, you will find that the procedures for selecting hole positions on the green vary. Greenkeepers or tournament organizers will often have different ideas in this respect, and an understanding of this will assist you.

The type of green design and playing difficulty will provide the options for hole position, and one concept is known as the triple six system, i.e. six easy, six medium-difficult, and six difficult pin positions. For professional events, this can be nine medium-hard and nine hard positions. A difficult hole position will require a precise approach shot and test all of your abilities once on the green. Knowing where the holes are going to be cut can greatly assist you.

When you are playing a practice round at a new course or playing an informal round at your own course, as well as putting toward the hole, putt towards different points on the green utilizing all of the possible positions for hole placement. This will better prepare you for the variety of putts you may face during a competition on the same greens.

Judging distance and lining up putts

Casual water

Sometimes when the ball comes to rest on the fringe of the green, although the lie may be good and dry, there may be casual water on the putting green between the ball and the hole. However, you are not permitted to take relief as the ball does not lie in or touching the casual water, nor does it interfere with your stance or the area of your intended swing. Assuming that you don't want to take a drop under a one-stroke penalty, you will have to chip the ball over the water with a lofted club.

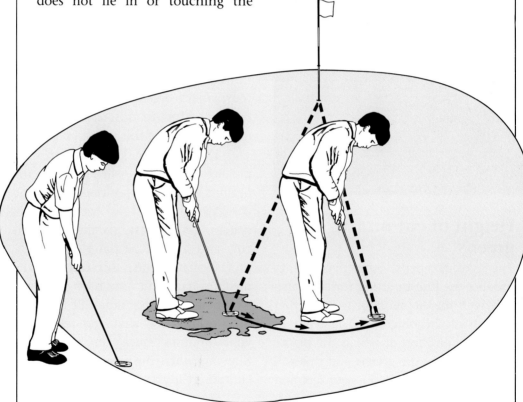

If your ball comes to rest in casual water on the putting surface itself, then you may obtain relief. Mark the point with a tee peg and pace the distance between that spot and the hole. You are entitled to replace your ball, not nearer the hole, but at a point nearest to where it lay which gives you maximum relief from the casual water.

Loose impediments

While you can adapt your putting to accommodate the natural elements, using your judgement skills, small debris on your putting line, such as leaves, stones and sand, cannot be contested by skill and a degree of luck will often prevail.

It is important that you understand what you are permitted to remove from your line and how to proceed accordingly. I therefore emphasise the importance of reading Rule 23 (Loose Impediments) contained in the Royal & Ancient Rules of Golf in conjunction with this section. It is not possible or practicable to remove all debris from your line, particularly on long putts, although in certain conditions it will be necessary to survey and clear the line on the short putts. This can become a lesser or greater task according to the season and general condition of the putting surface. On long putts, remove any debris that will clearly affect a rolling

On a short putt, you remove any loose impediments that might affect the roll. Pick them up with your hands – don't use the putter head. For longer breaking putts, consider your line at its widest point and remove any debris accordingly.

Judging distance and lining up putts

Pitch marks

You should erase a pitch mark using a special tool for the job. Insert the pitch fork around the perimeter of the pitch mark and gently raise, lifting inwards. Tap down with a putter – do not use your feet as the spikes in your shoes will make indentations and it is not permitted to erase spike marks on the green.

ball although do so to an extent that is practicable with due regard to time. On short putts of approximately six to eight feet, because you clearly expect to hole these you should place greater emphasis on removing as many loose impediments as possible, although again with discretion regarding time.

In addition to 'loose impediments' affecting putting line, it is also important to identify ball/pitch marks and repair them accordingly. You should refer to Rule 16 (The Putting Green) in order to establish how to proceed with regard to touching the line of putt.

While in the process of removing loose impediments from your line, take

Below: Cleaning impediments off the putter face. Even a small piece of grit on the face can put the ball off-line, i.e. like chalk on a snooker ball.

care not to transfer them on to your partner's line. For a putt that has a considerable break, it is important that you visualize clearly the journey the ball will take in order to clear its path of debris – for a straight putt, this is easy. Finally, while you are making your practice strokes during wet conditions, debris such as grass and leaves quite often gets stuck to the face of the putter, and from your viewpoint, looking downwards, this is not often visible. Remember to lift the putter before moving forward to address the ball, and either wipe the face with your finger or brush it across your trouser leg. This should be formulated as part of your pre-shot routine; a ball struck with debris on the putter face will often stop halfway to the hole.

The golf ball

Technology in equipment manufacturing is extremely advanced, especially the research and development of the golf ball. The type of ball you use can have an affect on your feel and subsequent ability to judge the speed of the greens. Golf balls that are generally targeted at the higher-handicap golfer are more durable than those designed for low-handicap and professional players. For example, a ball that has a two-piece construction and a surlyn cover will feel different to the hand and in playing characteristics than a wound ball with a balata cover. Surlyn is a resilient thermoplastic covering, and thus a two-piece ball construction will feel harder and will not spin as easily as its counterpart. Balata is a rubber

When you are experimenting with ball types there are three points to bear in mind.

1 Construction: Manufacturers will generally state whether the ball has a two- or three-piece construction, and the specific materials and their features within each section of construction.

2 Cover: Identify whether the cover is surlyn, balata or a blend of materials that are constantly under research and development.

3 Compression: This defines how much the ball will squeeze or compress under a specific load. The compression will clearly be stated and the lower the number the easier it will be to compress the ball. The recommended compression for you will depend on your normal swing speed and strength.

If you vary your ball type it can affect your feel and judgement as stated above, and I wish to emphasise finally that your choice of golf ball should be a consideration that takes your overall game into account.

substance, and a golf ball centre with a wound construction and a balata cover will feel different. It will spin more easily, and is not as durable as surlyn. Manufacturers have taken these two golf ball designs and expanded the possibilities by experimenting and correlating technology to produce a great many options in the choice of golf ball.

Judging distance and lining up putts

The wind, feel and touch

When considering how the various elements of weather affect your ability to putt, I believe that wind can have the most significant effect. Playing in hot temperatures requires, to a certain degree, additional fitness and concentration. Excessive rainfall, unlike light rain, will affect your putting stroke although at a certain stage in play would probably be abandoned. Frost conditions on the greens relegate skill to a mere lottery, and strong winds are the most difficult of all weather conditions to content with.

Putting in strong winds will affect every aspect that you normally take into account on the greens. Your balance and the length, strength and speed of your stroke will be affected including the line of putt. The key to your balance is the foundation that you establish at address; the stance and posture you adopt may require some adaptations in strong winds. Shorter putts, which you have a clear objective of holing, may require you to widen your stance and lower your posture to the ball until the wind force does not affect balance. This is equally important on long putts – if the wind is gusting into your back as you address the ball, sit back with more weight on your heels. Conversely, if it is blowing strongly towards your front, lean forwards with more weight towards the balls of your feet.

If the wind force is hard at you from the hole, lean your weight into your side that is closest to the hole. Therefore if it is blowing towards the hole, position a greater amount of weight accordingly. The most difficult aspect to control in these conditions is the putting stroke. Wind can, and often will, completely destroy your feel on the greens. It is not so much a case of the wind either slowing or increasing the speed of a rolling ball, although in excessive conditions this can happen,

but more a case of it completely overriding your sense and feel for the speed and strength of the stroke and dictating the terms to you.

At this extreme, putting in these conditions can become a lottery. When practising and playing in normal conditions you focus on the length, strength and path of the stroke, and you develop your feel accordingly. During strong

Putting

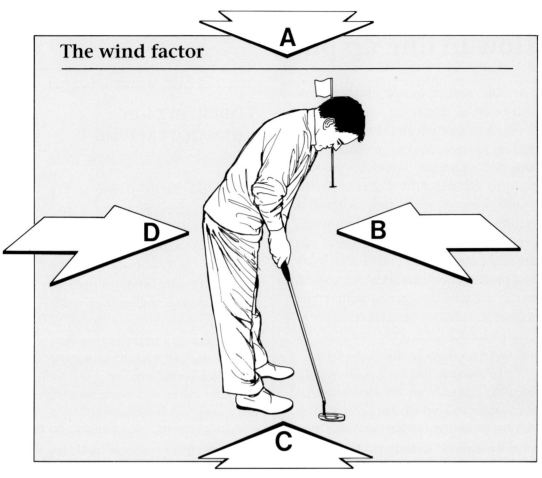

The wind factor

A strong wind blowing towards you from the hole (A) can increase the length of your backswing and affect your balance. Lean towards the hole. If a strong wind is blowing into your face (B), widen your stance and shift weight onto the balls of your feet. A wind force towards the hole (C) can shorten your backswing so position weight on your side facing away from the hole. If the wind is strong into your back (D), then position your weight more on your heels.

wind conditions blowing at you from the hole, you can feel the force of the wind override your senses and increase the length of your backswing which can lead you to subconsciously increase or decrease the speed of your through-swing. Conversely, a strong wind blowing toward the hole will have the effect of shortening your backswing and can likewise lead to an unintentional pass at the ball.

With this in mind, you can imagine how a forceful wind blowing into your back or at your front can distort the path of your putting stroke. Through pre-round practice on the putting green and observing your

playing partners, you can determine, if for example, a short straight putt may require aiming outside of the hole because in extremely forceful winds the line and roll of the ball will be affected.

There can be no hard and fast rules about putting in these conditions because clearly they will be too variable. Gripping your putter firmly and a clear awareness of these factors will help you to adapt accordingly. Finally, rather than be forced to experience these conditions during play, expose yourself to these elements on the putting green during practice to broaden your under-standing and ability to adapt to them when required.

Judging distance and lining up putts

How to line up putts

The skill required to line up your putts will be based largely on your ability to focus concentration and create a mental picture in your mind's eye. This can be acquired through various practice routines on the putting green. At the outset, spend as much time as possible on the practice green because although playing the course will be helpful, you are limited in the time you have to study and practise the elements of putting. To be a consistently good putter you require a sound stroke and an ability to create a mental picture that accounts for the variables that can affect the putt.

To read the line for a 30-foot putt, focusing carefully on the elements that can affect the result requires a large degree of concentration, and the first practice exercise is designed to develop that ability gradually be introducing a visualization process for short putts. I suggest that you practise each exercise for 20 to 30 minutes in order to maximize your concentration.

Align the manufacturer's name on the ball to the line you are going to take – not the hole. This is a very useful putting tip.

Visualizing line – practice exercise 1

Select a hole on the flattest part of the putting green and mark a position three feet from the hole giving yourself a straight putt. Putt a few balls into the hole until you have sensed the pace and strength of stroke required, and you are satisfied that there is no element of break. Take up a squatting position behind the ball looking along the line towards the hole.

The lower and more parallel you can establish your eyeline with the surface of the green the easier a visualization process will be. Therefore for this three-foot putt, position yourself 10 feet behind the ball.

This is now the crucial part of reading the line on your putts – remember, you know that this putt is perfectly straight. Look at the ball or marker and focus your eyeline to graduate along a straight line towards the hole, ensuring that as you start from the ball you focus intently on the grass along the line the ball has to follow straight to the hole centre. As your eyeline progresses forwards, focusing on the surface of the green, you will take into account automatically any change in the levels of the putting surface. This really is the essence of reading greens.

Proceed with this visualizing process for 30 seconds. Many club golfers who appear to go through a sound approach to reading line make many mistakes, and the appearance of an efficient routine will give you no indication that the player is staring *at* the line instead of *along* the line. You must focus on the marker and allow your eyeline to progress slowly forwards to the hole, in order that you can focus intently along every inch of the surface the ball has to cover to the centre of the hole.

Now move back four feet from the hole and continue the process. Putt a few balls into the hole to gauge the pace and the strength and speed of stroke required, and again stop and spend a few seconds creating the mental picture outlined above. Continue moving back at one-foot increments and you will gradually develop the ability to concentrate for greater periods and visualize the ball rolling for longer distances.

Select a three-foot straight line and putt a few balls into the hole. Now position yourself 10 feet behind the ball and get your eyeline parallel to the green's surface. For a few seconds, you graduate your eyeline towards the hole. Increase the distance to four feet and repeat.

87

Judging distance and lining up putts

The visualization process – practice exercise 2

Select a three-foot putt on the practice green that contains an element of break, either left to right or vice versa. Putt a few balls towards the hole not allowing for any break at this point. Observe at which point along the line the ball breaks and by how much it has moved by the time it reaches a point level with the hole. Assuming that you are practising a left-to-right putt begin to allow for the break by progressively aiming left of the hole until you sense the line and pace. After you have holed a few more balls and clearly pictured the line, then stop. Position yourself behind the ball as described above and spend 30 seconds creating a mental picture by focusing your eyeline to progress along the path the putts had taken to find the hole. Continue in accordance with the previous exercise.

As you increase the distance for 'break' putts using this exercise, you may find that the line and margin of break changes and this will further develop your concentration to focus on different break runs and longer distances. Now position yourself on the opposite side of the hole to develop the same awareness for putts with a right-to-left break, again commencing from three feet.

The learning concept of exercises 1 and 2

During the exercises for straight and break putts you were asked first to putt balls at the hole to identify the line, and then having established that in your mind's eye, to take up a position behind the ball and create a mental picture of the ball rolling along the appropriate line. Using this concept, you will quickly develop your ability to visualize putting line, because clearly it is easier to create a mental picture of something that you have just seen. In this case, you establish the actual line and then recreate it immediately through visualization. Practise the two exercises to sharpen your visual ability, and the next exercise will test your concentration to read the line before you putt.

CHAPTER SIX

Reading the greens

by Nick Allen

Estimating the speed

Understanding the green-keeping activities you see constantly as you play will prove a significant advantage for your improvement on the putting surface. There is a perceptible change in the speed of a green after mowing. This can vary according to the height of cut although sometimes this is not clearly visible to the eye. Learning the mowing schedules of your green-keeping team will keep you aware of changing conditions.

If, for example, you are aware of the speed of the greens on a specific course, and you are playing a practice round during the morning of the day before the event, knowing whether the greens are going to be cut that afternoon, the following morning, or not at all, will help you determine how they will play. A good example of how conditions can change in the same day is the procedure sometimes adopted at major championships where the greens are mowed twice a day. Two further practices that will require your awareness are top dressing and verti-cutting. Both will create faster putting surfaces and it is important that you identify these activities. When the greens are top-dressed and the soil is worked into the putting surface it is sometimes not clearly noticeable, but it will smooth the surface and quicken the pace.

Verti-cutting is the process whereby a series of knives approximately three inches long penetrate the grass to reduce its density, which subsequently will increase putting speed.

Reading the greens

Grass types

Knowing how to identify the basic grass types used on greens will enable you to quickly establish how they will play. This will become increasingly more important as you visit more courses. In general, the greens on more established courses predominantly contain annual meadow grass which is a coarser broad-leaf grass. Many new course developments are using creeping bent grasses, and the different putting conditions both types produce are significant. Creeping bent grass is a fine narrow-leaf grass, and a close look can detect the difference between this and annual meadow grass. The creeping bent type offers a quick putting surface requiring a greater allowance for break, whereas the broad-leaf annual meadow gives a perceptible slower surface.

Bents and fescue grasses are more readily found on links courses and usually provide a quicker putting surface.

The hand-cut greens at Woodbridge Golf Club, Suffolk. The lines denote that they have been cut by hand. The grass is a very fine fescue which produces an ideal putting surface for fast-pace greens, and tends to be faster than the coarser broad-leaf meadow grass on some courses.

Green location

It was mentioned earlier that whereas 18 greens may have similar characteristics during normal conditions, their recovery from different weather conditions may vary and it is important that you understand this.

New green construction

If a new green is constructed on an established course a number of factors may contribute to a change in putting conditions compared to the existing greens. The construction specification may have varied from the original greens, thereby producing a faster or slower drainage process after rain. The grass type may be different which can produce a significant change in putting speed. Moreover, during the establishing period after construction, the putting surface will be in a transitional stage.

Remember that greens with contours and high and low levels may recover differently after rain, and therefore specific sections within the same green can affect putting speed and break – this should be considered for long putts. Remain aware of these factors, observe the location of greens, their design and how adverse weather will affect playing conditions and you will find it easier to adapt to changing conditions.

Location

Greens located in dense trees or hollows can produce problems for both the greenkeeper and for you, the golfer. A green enclosed by trees that block out sunlight, will take longer to recover from rain and frost, and excessive debris may be deposited from the trees creating further problems. A green located in a hollow may have a slower rate of recovery from frost, and steep banking around the green may create a run of water on to the surface after rainfall.

The green in the foreground is flat and exposed, whereas the green in the background is in the shade of the trees and therefore will tend to have a slower pace than the green in front of it.

Reading the greens

How to read break

With practice you will quickly develop the ability to focus your concentration and visualize a straight line to the hole, but to create a mental picture of the line on a break putt is rather more difficult. There is no exact science to determine how a ball will react to the contours on a green because of the many variables we have discussed. The simple fact is that the more you practise and study the greens on your own course, the more proficient you will become at negotiating difficult putts.

You will face putts that contain a subtle element of break requiring careful evaluation, and also putts that are obvious with regard to which side of the hole the ball will break. The difficult factor to determine is what margin to borrow, and the strength and speed of stroke required to achieve the necessary curvature to the hole.

There was an underlying reason during an earlier practice exercise that will assist your progress on reading break. You were asked to focus carefully on the grass as you graduated your eye-line slowly toward the hole for straight putts. Remember that this process allows you automatically to take into account a change of level on the putting surface to determine at what point the ball may break from a straight line. Many golfers having positioned themselves behind the ball immediately attempt to visualize how the ball will curve and break. You will learn to do this eventually, but it is important initially that you visualize the ball rolling on a straight line towards the hole. This allows you to determine at what point and by how much the ball will 'break' from the straight line. This realisation will act as a catalyst for you to gauge and picture the margin of borrow required.

Practice exercise

Select a six-foot putt on a sloping section of the putting green. Place four balls around the hole in positions that each contain a different break. Four balls will be sufficient because of the concentration required for this exercise.

Position yourself 10 feet behind the ball with your eye-line as low as possible. Although clearly there will be a need to allow for break, establish the reaction if you chose a straight line and allow the feedback to create a visualization process for the amount of borrow needed. Practise this exercise for 20 minutes.

Above: The three tee pegs on the left indicate the slope and break. In between the second and third tee pegs is the point of break.

Reading the greens

Pace and borrow

The key to judging distance with the correct pace is to make full use of your practice strokes to simulate the strength and speed of stroke required. Continually rolling medium and long putts either short or beyond the hole, to an extent that requires you to again mark the ball and read the line, will create pressure. Imagine that you had a 15-foot right-to-left putt with a 12-inch break, and you over-borrowed aiming two feet left of the hole and then underhit the putt. The likely result could be a three-foot putt with the same degree of break and concentration required.

The player in this example over-borrowed and yet many golfers wrongly conclude that they have misread the line when in fact all they have done is fail to remain positive with the original line chosen. Golfers will often study and select the line, step up to address the ball, and the different perspective they see from the address position can create doubt leading to under-hit putts and sometimes a change of mind during the motion of the stroke. Be aware of this deception and stay faithful to your chosen line.

Continually rolling putts either short of or past the hole to a degree that requires marking and reading will place unwanted pressure on you. If you had a 15-foot right-to-left putt with a 12-inch break and proceeded to overborrow by aiming two feet wide of the hole, and then underhit the putt, you would have to mark and read another break putt.

The hole is your secondary target

Consider the different skill elements involved when holing a 10-foot putt that is straight, and one with a considerable break. Although a simplified statement, the straight putt would require a correctly weighted stroke, delivered squarely along the target line as it strikes the ball. On the perfect surface you would hole this putt every time. Conversely the demands for holing the break putt are greater. Having read the line and determined the extent of borrow, you must aim your putter wide

Left: A straight putt to the back of the hole where stance, alignment and the putter head are aimed at the centre of the hole, and pace is the important factor. The last three balls show how the break has taken place. Perfect pace allows this to happen. If the putt was struck too strongly, the break would not take effect until the ball had passed the hole. If understruck, it would finish short and left of the hole.

Above: Here we can see that the slope on the green requires a two-foot borrow. The player is standing and aiming two feet right of the hole as is the blade.

of the hole and the stroke must be weighted perfectly to roll the ball along the line at the perfect speed, allowing the contours to shape the curvature of the rolling ball inwards to the hole.

On the straight putt the hole is your primary target, but it is the secondary target for the break putt. Your priority is to roll the ball accurately along your chosen line at the right speed and then, if the line was correctly chosen, the hole becomes a factor. This emphasises again the importance of trusting your line.

Reading the greens

Pace and weight over borrow

When you strike a putt, the speed of the rolling ball will influence how the contours will affect the break. Pace and borrow are thereby related. A putt can be holed by choosing more than one line, but the consequences of missing the hole and the return putt must be considered. Try the following simple exercise to demonstrate how pace will overcome break.

Weight over borrow exercise

1 Select a four-foot putt with a degree of break and read the line in the usual way. Putt a few balls until you have confirmed the break and curvature by holing a few.
2 Now ignore the break entirely and putt a few balls on a straight line. Gradually increase the strength of your stroke until the speed of the ball overrides the break.

Sidehill putts

Fast-breaking sidehill putts will also require an awareness of the 'safe' area for the subsequent putt. The key to controlling them is to allow the slope to do the work and not the ball.

Sidehill exercise

Select a 15- to 20-foot right-to-left putt that contains a significant break. Without studying line, putt a few balls straight at the hole and then progressively increase the margin of borrow to the right.

The object of this exercise is to enhance your awareness of the amount of borrow sometimes necessary in order to control the speed of the ball. It is very easy to under-borrow and strike these putts too hard. It may appear impossible to leave the ball close although understanding the extent of borrow sometimes necessary will enable you to achieve good results. The previous exercise showed you how pace overcomes borrow. The exact opposite is the key in this case.

As the ball slows down, notice how the slope has a greater influence on the break; in fact, the greater margin you borrow the more the ball, will move sideways as it slows, down the slope toward the hole, (This, of course, will depend on the extremity of the slope.)

It is precisely this line that you should identify, and then

continue to observe the reaction of the ball.

Notice how it will pass a specific point on your line, and the curvature of the roll moves sideways as it first slows and then gains momentum from the slope as it moves towards the hole. Practise right-to-left and left-to-right putts.

Reading the greens

Uphill putts

On many putts that contain break a ball left two-and-a-half feet from the hole yet on the wrong side may be less preferable than a five-foot straight putt slightly uphill. Depending on the severity of the slope, remain aware of the consequences of being too bold on uphill putts.

Uphill two-tiered green

Most golfers leave these putts short of the hole because they become preoccupied in negotiating the middle section of the putt (the gradient of the tier) yet fail to account for the first and third stages: the ball must be struck firm enough to cover the lower level, the tier itself, and retain sufficient speed to run out to the hole. The following exercise will broadly test your judgement ability for these putts.

Exercise 1

On the bottom level place a tee peg six feet from the gradient and three more at nine, twelve and 15 feet. Place a tee peg six feet beyond the tier on the top level. From the bottom level, putt three balls towards the target marker from each distance – your ability to adapt judgement will be tested as you increase distance.

Exercise 2

On the bottom level, leave the tees at six, nine, twelve and 15 feet and on the top level, starting at four feet, increase the distance to eight, twelve and sixteen feet. Start at six feet from the bottom level and putt three balls toward the four-foot marker. By increasing distance along the lower and upper levels you will develop your touch for these putts.

Downhill putts
Two tier

If the hole was positioned on the lower level 10 feet from a tier with a six-foot gradient and your ball was 20 feet back on the top level, your ability to judge pace over the first stage would be crucial. The pace of the ball would almost have to stop as it reaches the slope allowing the momentum from this point to roll the ball down to the hole. Conversely if you were putting close to the downslope from the upper level towards a hole position 30 feet away on the lower level, the strength of stroke would need to account for the slope and the length over the lower level.

Reading the greens

Exercise 1

Place a target tee marker on the bottom level six feet from the slope. Place tee pegs on the top at six, twelve and 18 feet from the edge. At each increasing distance, this exercise will test your feel over the first stage of the putt. The speed over each distance of the first stage may have to slow considerably allowing the momentum from the slope to roll the ball down to the hole.

Exercise 2

This exercise will test your ability to adapt your judgement over increasing distances on the lower and upper levels. Position tee pegs away from the slope at six, twelve and 18 feet on both the lower and upper levels. Starting from six feet on the upper level, putt three balls from each distance marker and observe the change of strength required to pace the ball accurately to the corresponding marker on the lower level.

Undulating putts

A putt that contains a series of undulations requires a process of elimination to determine how each slope may affect speed. An important factor is to observe the distance between the final slope and the hole and decide how the momentum gained from here will affect the run out to the hole. If possible, on the putting green select an undulating putt, and on the flat section just beyond the final mound place a series of markers to test your judgement.

Reading the greens

Set the ball in motion

You will face certain downhill putts on extremely fast greens where any element of weight in the stroke would send the ball well past the hole should you miss. As the heading suggests it may be sufficient to do no more than set the ball in motion allowing the momentum gained from the slope to provide the pace. Practise these putts and remember that for all downhill putts you should be aware of a sufficient pace necessary to leave the ball beyond the hole should you miss the first putt.

Study the distance between the final mound and the hole and then determine what effect the momentum gained from the downslope will have on the run to the hole. If possible, on the practice green place markers on the flat section beyond the final mound to test your ability.

Factors affecting speed and break

Grain

Grain will have a significant effect on speed and break in hot climates where a coarse grass, such as Bermuda, is sown. A growth habit of Bermuda, in addition to the mowing patterns, can encourage these thicker grass leaves to lean in a particular direction that will affect speed and break accordingly.

A down-grain putt where the grass leaves lean towards the hole will tend to be faster, but if pressed towards you, the putting speed will be slower. Quite often there is a distinct shine to the surface of a down-grain putt, versus a dull appearance putting against the grain.

The effect of grain on break

If you have a straight putt where grain runs across the line, it may be necessary to aim outside of the hole accordingly. Should you have a left-to-right or right-to-left break where the grain runs in the opposite direction, you will need to judge what effect the grain could have on the break, and decide the margin you borrow accordingly. Obviously the weight of your stroke will also be a factor and in this regard to the weight over borrow exercise.

Straight putts with the grain are very fast whereas putts against the grain are very slow. The down-grain has a shiny effect on the grass with it lying flat and away from you. The up-grain grass is against you. The effect is more difficult to establish when the putt is sideways to the grain and it can have a startling effect on the break of the ball.

Reading the greens

Plumb-bobbing

Right: Squat right behind the ball and look along the line from the ball to the hole.

If you play regularly on a particular course you will familiarize yourself with the speed and contours over a period of time. However, if you visit a new course, judgement may prove more difficult. Putts that are read from the usual position looking towards the hole sometimes indicate a completely different line when viewed from behind the hole looking back towards the ball. Having taken a positive decision on line it is vital to remain faithful and support your choice.

Plumb-bobbing is an excellent method that can reconcile any doubt and identify the break on contours that are subtle and sometimes difficult to see by eye.

The concept
Either stand or crouch behind the ball holding the putter between thumb and forefinger. Extend your arm to allow the putter to 'hang' vertically, holding the putter at the bottom of the grip.

In plumb-bobbing, as you can see, the angle of the putter is vertical and the toe is pointing toward the hole.

It is vital that the putter 'hangs' in a vertical position, as if the putter head is wrongly positioned your judgement can become distorted. Make sure that the toe of the putter points directly at the hole. Position yourself directly behind the ball, and extend your arm forwards allowing the putter to hang vertically. Focus your eye-line to position the vertical shaft line so that it bisects the ball and the hole.

If the hole appears to the right of the shaft line a left-to-right contour is indicated and vice versa. Where the shaft line perfectly bisects the ball and hole, a straight putt is indicated.

When you are in doubt or reading greens that contain subtle contour, the plumb-bobbing method can eliminate doubt and identify line.

Sound putting management

Finally, I would like to offer some general ideas that you can include in your routines and approach to putting. They provide an insight for sound planning and preparation.

The greens on some courses have particular design characteristics, or natural landform or the motives of the designer may prevail. It is important to practise the predominant putt you are likely to face if, for example, the course had a tendency towards two-tiered greens. When preparing for a competition and playing a practice round at a new course, it can be a significant advantage to know where the holes could be positioned, or if all the greens have similar playing characteristics. Talk to the professional, the greenkeeper or members; make notes and file any information gained for further reference.

Effective time management on the green

Although we have discussed reading line from the usual position facing the hole, where time permits it is clearly an advantage to survey line from the side and behind the hole looking back to the ball. If you are playing in a two-, three- or four-ball, as you approach the green determine when it is your turn to putt. If you are last to putt, promptly mark your ball and clean it taking your usual position to read line while the first player prepares to putt. As the first player strikes his putt, move to a side view and survey your line as the second player prepares to putt, progressing finally to view the putt from behind the hole as the final player prepares. Many golfers waste time in this situation, sometimes

While the first player prepares to putt, the second and third players are both studying their line.

Reading the greens

As you walk to the green, observe when it is your turn to putt. If you are playing in a three- or fourball, using your time efficiently can give you the opportunity to study the line from more than one angle.

leaning on the putter awaiting their turn. Obviously it is important to consider your movements with due regard to your partner's line and concentration. Managing your time effectively and thorough preparation will lead to increased confidence on the greens. A putt missed or holed on the first green can have an effect on confidence throughout the round.

If you are last to putt on the first green make sure you study the reaction of your partner's putts to assist your cause. As you walk round the course, note where the pins are positioned on subsequent holes to be played. This will assist club selection and, if appropriate, an awareness of the ideal section of green from which to putt.

Summary

I believe these concepts will increase your understanding of the numerous elements affecting your ability to putt, and additionally the putting stroke you will develop will lead to a significant improvement on the greens leading to lower scores.

CHAPTER SEVEN

Great putts

by Martin Vousden

The greatest putts need not necessarily be the longest. It is circumstance and setting that dictate the importance or greatness of a putt, not merely its length. There are occasions when a sidehill breaking four footer is worth considerably more recognition and praise than a 50-foot monster across the width of a green. Almost without exception, major championships and other tournaments are decided on the putting surface – there have been very few instances where someone has chipped in to claim victory.

So it is the greens that most cruelly expose the strengths and frailties of the golfer. If a player has a six-foot putt to win, and all the time in the world to stalk it, study it and worry about it, his nerve and stroke will be examined minutely for any sign of hesitancy or weakness. It is no coincidence that the careers of many great players – people like Ben Hogan, Sam Snead, Tony Jacklin and Peter Alliss – have been brought prematurely to a competitive end because of an inability to continue putting with conviction. Alliss and Jacklin are still regarded as among the best ball strikers in Britain but both were obliged to find other careers in golf when a smooth putting stroke deserted them. They represent only a tiny percentage of the misery that this most frustrating element of a frustrating game can bring.

Most of us spend our lives chasing, and sometimes achieving, our ambitions, but it falls on few of us to have one single moment when all that we have worked for over decades can be achieved, or lost, in an instant. However, it is in the nature of many sports, and golf in particular, that 20 or 25 years of work, sacrifice, struggle and, eventually, achievement can be focused into one putt – one moment in which a career can be celebrated and fêted, or relegated forever into the 'not quite good enough' category. So the next time you see a professional golfer stand over a six footer, with the knowledge that it is: 'This to win the tournament', rather than be surprised if he should miss, consider it a miracle should it be holed.

Great putts

Monster of St Andrews

In the 1990 Open Championship at St Andrews, a young American, Mike Allen, sank what probably was the longest putt ever seen on that historic links. By conservative estimates, Allen's golf ball travelled 100 feet across the 13th green before hitting the back of the cup so hard that it leapt two feet in the air before dropping with a clatter.

Yet although this was a remarkable putt, it was not a great one because it fulfilled only one of the three criteria demanded for greatness. These are: occasion, tension and significance.

The occasion was important enough but tension was notable by its absence – largely because it was the first day of the championship and, although Allen shot a joint best-of-the-day-66, the big players had yet to make their moves and many an aspiring champ has led the first day of a major tournament never to be heard of again. Because of this, significance was also lacking. It was clear that the young American was having a good day but that was all.

Tiddler at Augusta

Contrast Mike Allen's experience with the six-foot putt sunk by Ian Woosnam on the final green of the Augusta National course during the 1991 Masters.

Woosnam had led the tournament for most of the last day, knowing, as only professional golfers can, the inexorable tightening of the screw of tension that a five-hour competitive round of golf brings. Not only that, he was playing alongside Tom Watson, an eight-times winner of golf's major tournaments, and one of the most personable and popular figures of the modern game. In consequence, unfortunately Woosnam's poor shots (particularly a pulled drive on the 13th) were cheered almost as loudly as Watson's great ones.

The two men arrived on the 18th green in joint share of the lead and Woosnam eventually stood over the putt that he knew would make him Masters champion if he holed it, or also-ran if he missed – perhaps, like Tom Kite, destined to wear the albatross label around his neck of 'The Greatest Player in the World never to Win a Major'.

Fallible Welshman

In addition to all this, Woosnam has a somewhat inconsistent putting stroke. Watching him on the greens is akin to closing your eyes before crossing the road – an experience made doubly exciting by its sheer unpredictability.

If Woosnam had a putting action like Nick Faldo, Ben Crenshaw, or Colin Montgomerie, he would, when on form, be virtually unbeatable. In truth, he battered his way to the top of the Sony World Rankings despite, not because of, his ability on the greens. And here he stood on a golf course that was one of the most notorious in the world for the speed and trickiness of its putting surfaces.

He is not a bad putter – no one could climb as high in the game as he has if that were so – but he is and probably always will be the epitome of inconsistency. Some days he holes everything in sight with an insouciant ease, whereas on others he cannot putt into a bucket.

One of the oldest games among golf watchers is to decide which player they would nominate if a five footer had to be holed and your life depended on it. In any such poll it is a fair bet that the name at the top of the list would not be Woosnam.

Added pressure

Yet if all that were not enough, the Welshman had set his stall out before the tournament began by saying that he badly wanted to win and now was the time to claim a major. For the previous five years, as he climbed to ascendancy, first in Europe and then in the rest of the world, he asserted with ever-increasing certainty that he was not interested in major championships, only financial security.

However, a few weeks before Augusta he about-faced, declaring that his hunger to win the game's greatest honours was as great as anyone's. He had, he said, been suggesting disinterest simply to reduce expectations and pressure. But now was the time to reveal the extent of his golfing ambitions, he added, and find out just how good he was. This desire was to be satisfied sooner than even he, perhaps, thought.

There was no doubt that the three criteria defining a great putt were all in evidence as he addressed his ball on the 72nd green of the '91 Masters. The occasion was one of the greatest in golf; the first major of the season and the only one to be played at the same magical venue every year.

Tension existed in abundance, as it always does over the closing holes at Augusta. Finally, there was significance. As Ian Woosnam lined up his putt he knew with absolute certainty that he was about to play the most important golf shot of the many millions he had struck in his career to date.

Short but sweet

In customary style, he spent little time fussing and fiddling about; he took his usual quick look at the line from both ends, settled over the ball and struck it firmly. He knew it was good before it even reached the hole and sank almost to his right knee, fist clenched in triumph and relief as the ball travelled the last couple of feet into the cup. That was a great putt.

Great putts

The shark strikes

If Ian Woosnam was at the top of the world golfing tree in 1991, Greg Norman, 'The Great White Shark', was one of the contenders for that title in 1984.

The strengths of his game were, and always have been, apparent. He not only hit the ball huge distances but he usually, unlike other impressive strikers, knew where it was going. Many players hit the ball a long way. Many others are robotically accurate but there have been few who are as straight and long as Norman.

Allied to this contained power is a putting stroke which, when on song, is the equal of anyone in the world for its simplicity and, more important, its effectiveness. Norman could, and still does, string together birdies with incomparable ease.

Birdie blitz

No better example of his prodigious scoring abilities could be seen than at the 1989 Open Championship at Royal Troon. Norman started the day seven strokes off the lead and was clearly destined to finish well down the leader board – except that no-one told him.

He launched one of his customary last-day charges by birdieing the first six holes, shooting 64 and clawing himself into a three-way playoff with Wayne Grady and eventual champion Mark Calcavecchia. Norman's birdie blitz looked set to come unstuck when he found the green at the fifth hole but he

could hardly have been further away from the flag, about 45 feet. Yet he rolled that monster in as calmly as he had potted the considerably shorter putts he had faced on each of his first four holes.

After such stirring deeds it was especially sad for Norman to drive 325 yards on the last playoff hole (Troon's 18th), into a bunker which he said he had simply not taken into consideration, believing it outside his range.

Putting

Everything to play for

In 1984, when the US Open visited Wing Foot, Norman was an awesomely talented young man with an unlimited golfing future. He lived up to all those expectations by finishing on 276, in a tie for first place, with Fuzzy Zoeller.

This alone was cause to praise him but the manner in which he booked his playoff place was what really got the fans excited. He played the 18th ahead of Zoeller, knowing that he needed a par four to probably tie.

After a good drive he pushed his approach shot well right – a weakness under pressure that was to be spotlighted cruelly at Augusta and in the US PGA in subsequent years. From a horrible position in the rough, Norman had no chance of putting backspin on the ball and watched with increasing anxiety as it rolled ever further across

Great putts

the green, eventually coming to a stop nearly 50 feet past the flag, just off the back of the green.

A study in concentration

Watching videotape of Norman as he stalked that putt, there is no doubting the tension etched into his features as he told himself that he must hole it to stay alive in the championship – and no doubt tried to put the previous two shots out of his mind. He is normally a fairly quick and decisive player but this time he studied the green, the lie of his ball, the nap of the grass and the slope of the putting surface in apparently micro-scopic detail – as well he might.

The major factor was undoubtedly the slope of the green; it was generally reckoned that Norman's ball would move 10 feet from left to right on its journey to the hole, but even experi-enced pros have difficulty in sometimes convincing themselves that what they see is real.

To read a green at any time and then strike the golf ball several feet away from where you want it to go, confident in your ability to determine the slope so that you know the ball will find its even-tual destination, takes judgement and a certain act of faith. To rely on that judgement to the exclusion of all else, on the most important golfing day of your life, requires guts and character every bit as much as judgement and ability.

Slow journey

Greg Norman proved himself equal to the task. For the first half of his golf

ball's seemingly endless journey he looked simply anxious. Then, as it slowed pace a little and began to swing right towards the hole, he began to follow it, allowing the first hint of a smile and relief to ease the tension of his features. As it travelled its last few feet before dropping into the cup, he was walking after it, putter raised in the air with his left hand, almost as if to conduct the slowly rising cheers of the massed gallery which was now urging the ball on with increasing urgency and excitement.

Waving the flag

Finally it fell, to a resounding cheer that could probably be heard all over the golf course. It could certainly be heard 200 yards away down the fairway, where Fuzzy Zoeller, waiting to play his approach shot, assumed that the roar signalled a birdie and, in one of the most gracious sporting gestures of the last decade, waved his white towel in mock surrender.

Twenty four hours later, Norman reciprocated the gesture as, with his customary forbearance he accepted his defeat in the playoff, having shot a disappointing 75 to Zoeller's excellent 67. The final act of the '84 US Open belonged to the American but the previ-ous day had just as emphatically been Norman's, thanks to that putt.

All in a row

Great putting, like most other elements of golf, is a gift given to only a few. Some players, like Ben Crenshaw and Bobby Locke, are consistently above the rest.

Others, such as Ben Hogan and Sam Snead, have greatness on their shoulders for a few fragile years but once it leaves, find themselves reduced to being only a shadow of the superb players they once were.

Others still are good, steady putters who, for a few rounds, weeks or months at a time, are blessed by an uncanny streak of ability that allows them to hole virtually every ball. For this reason, great putts often come in a batch, and it is as if the confidence the player gets from holing one gives him better vision with which to see the line and better ability to stroke the ball along that line at the right speed.

This is why we see players like Greg Norman at Royal Troon making six birdies in a row.

Nicklaus swansong

A similar hot streak was enjoyed by Jack Nicklaus during the 1986 US Masters. He is the most successful player in the history of golf, having won either 18 or 20 major championships (depending on whether you include two US Amateur titles as majors).

He had three Opens, four US Opens and five US PGAS and US Masters each to his name. Since the early 1960s he bestrode the game like no other player, in terms of performance and longevity. But his best days were inevitably behind him as he teed up at Augusta at the age of 46 – four years older than any previous winner. His last major triumph had been in 1980, when he took both the US Open and US PGA titles, and his fifth success in the Masters had been 11 years earlier in 1975.

No great expectations

The crowds enjoyed seeing Nicklaus and wished him well but no-one really expected him to win. After the first three days that pessimistic view was confirmed when the 'Golden Bear' shot 74, 71, 69 to earn a shared ninth place going into the final round. His relegation to the role of supporting player seemed confirmed after he played the front nine in 35 (one under par), and it was only a birdie at the ninth that allowed him to enter red numbers.

But that birdie was the first of three consecutive ones which awoke the scoreboard attendants, and the galleries. The buzz went round the course: 'Jack is back' and everybody rushed to watch him.

By the time many of them reached him, however, his momentum was stopped by a bogey four at the notoriously difficult par three 12th. Yet their expectations rose again as the great man birdied hole 13. Mind you, he was expected to because the par 5s at Augusta are considered to be the key to scoring well in the Masters.

Great finish

A routine par at the 14th led a few dispirited souls to wander away in search of other excitement but Nicklaus

Great putts

was not finished with them, or the tournament, just yet. He then played the next three holes in 3,2,3 (against a par of 5,3,4), picking up four strokes with an eagle, birdie, birdie charge that put him right back in contention.

Of those sub-par holes, the one that most people remember is the 17th, where a slippery, downhill 12-footer seemed almost predestined to go right in the hole. At least that's what Nicklaus thought because he raised his putter in his left hand and walked towards the

hole long before the ball had dropped. The smile on his face told the world that he had not only played the back nine in a six-under-par 30, but had hoisted himself into strong contention.

All he could do now was to sit back in the clubhouse to see if another player would hold his nerve down Augusta's infamous back nine. Neither Greg Norman, Seve Ballesteros or Tom Kite could do so, leaving Nicklaus to be helped into a green jacket for the sixth time.

Faldo's finale

Augusta National was also the venue for one of Nick Faldo's greatest triumphs when the anguish of a two-year search to rebuild his swing was finally vindicated as he took the green jacket in two consecutive years.

Always one of the putting greats, Faldo decided that his full swing could not live up to the rigours imposed on it by the pressure of the last day in a Major. He consequently went through one of the most publicized rebuilding programmes in golf. He reaped the rewards in 1987 at The Open in Muirfield, shooting 18 straight pars on the final day in poor weather for what has been described as the 'perfect' round of golf.

Yet for a man of Faldo's talent and ambition, one major would never be enough and he set about adding to his tally with the same rigorous and meticulous attention to detail that he had shown in refining his swing. So considered was his approach that some commentators wrongly suggested that he played only four tournaments a year, the majors, and that all the others were simply practice.

World leader

In 1989 he arrived at Augusta as one of the leading players in the world – having taken Curtis Strange to a US Open playoff the previous summer – and strongly fancied, not least because of his silky putting stroke.

Augusta National is famed for many things but what has set its reputation above all else is the speed and difficulty of its greens. To win there takes a lot of qualities but one of the first attributes that needs to be pencilled in to a would-be victor's curriculum vitae is: 'Excellent putter.' Faldo is exactly that. For about a year after he arrived on Tour with his new swing it worked perfectly but he could not buy a putt. It seemed that he had spent so long perfecting one part of his game that the area he could always rely on had rusted due to neglect. Now, with a lot of hard time on the practice green, he was back to his velvet best.

Long way to go

Like Nicklaus in 1986, Faldo entered the final day of the 1989 Masters a fair way back – five shots to be precise. Included among the many names ahead of him on the leader board were four previous winners: Tom Watson, Larry Mize, Ben Crenshaw and Seve Ballesteros. It seemed possible that Faldo could overhaul some but surely not all? And as he started the final round he was not in the best of moods.

The third round had been delayed by rain and many players were forced to complete it on the final day. Faldo had to come out early to play five holes, hoped to complete them in two under par and played them in two over instead.

The final round itself did not start well either. Faldo played steady golf to

Great putts

put himself three strokes behind the leaders after 14 holes. But then the putter really got going and birdies at 15, 16 and 17 dragged him right up in the action. Of those three putts, the middle one, on the 16th, was probably the most crucial.

History repeats

His tee shot had come to rest about 15 feet from the hole, just off the green but, even more critically, above the flag. Of all the priorities at Augusta, placing the ball below the hole, leaving an uphill putt, is one of the most important. The shot facing Faldo was almost identical to the one tackled by Sandy Lyle a year before except that there was mud stick-

ing to Faldo's ball which he could not wipe off because it was not on the putting surface.

He said later: "I couldn't believe how I could hole that one. It was 15 feet but there must have been seven or eight feet of break on it and I just touched it like I would a two-foot putt."

Like Lyle's ball 12 months earlier, Faldo's took all that left-to-right break and dived into the hole at a speed which suggested that, had it not dropped, it would have rolled clear off the green.

A couple of hours later, in near darkness, Faldo holed a 25-footer on the second playoff hole to beat Scott Hoch and claim his first green jacket but it was the knee-knocker on the 16th that had got him there.

Medinah magic

Many testing putts have been holed on the final green in a major championship; many other long ones have also been buried. But few great, long putts have disappeared into the 72nd hole when it really counted. One that did, and will always be remembered, was struck by Hale Irwin at the last hole of regulation play during the 1990 Open at Medinah Country Club.

The putt was extraordinary, the player's reaction even more so because Irwin launched himself on a triumphant, jubilant lap of honour halfway round the green, slapping palms with marshals and spectators alike. Yet the tournament leaders were still two hours away, having just finished their front nine, so how could Irwin be so sure that his putt was of such great significance?

The tough get going

One of the reasons was his experience. When it came to national championships, Irwin had been there before, having claimed the US Open title at Winged Foot in 1974, and Inverness, Ohio, in 1979. If these two venues had anything in common, it was their sheer uncompromising toughness, and Irwin had a reputation to match. He was a meticulously straight hitter, particularly with long irons but, like most of the greats, his most effective weapon was his brain. He rarely made foolish mistakes and, if given the opportunity, would be as tough as needed to get the job done.

Dark horse

However, as the championship opened, Irwin was on none of the pundits' lists as a potential winner. He was 45 years old and his second US Open win had been 11 years earlier. His last victory of any kind had been the 1985 Memorial and his form going into Medinah did not suggest a staggering resurgence of that old magic.

In fact, he was only in the field thanks to a special invitation from the championship organisers, the United States Golf Association. Irwin's 10-year exemption from qualifying (as a previous champion) had expired so he faced the humiliating prospect of having to tee up with a bunch of unknowns over 36 holes in order to have another crack at the title. The USGA only offered one special invitation in 1990 but they offered it wisely.

Confident

During the practice days at Medinah, Irwin was as relaxed and confident as anyone could be under such circumstances. He had finished third at the Kemper Open two weeks before and had then taken a week off, so he was refreshed but in good form.

More importantly, perhaps, the course was a tough one and the second longest on the US Open rota. It therefore called for a lot of approach shots to be played with long irons – the greatest playing weapons in Irwin's considerable armoury. However, the front-runners

Great putts

were players like Curtis Strange (going for three US Opens in a row) and Nick Faldo who, as reigning Masters champion, was the only man who could do the 'Grand Slam' of four majors in a season.

Laying the foundation

Irwin, meanwhile, did what he does best. He played a beast of a course in as quiet and unassuming a manner as possible for three-and-a-half days. Going into the final round he was on a total of 213, four strokes behind the joint leaders and relative unknowns Mike Donald and Billy Ray Brown. In between were players like Larry Nelson, Fuzzy Zoeller, Nick Faldo, Curtis Strange and Jose-Maria Olazabal.

Yet it was Irwin's playing partner, Greg Norman, who grabbed the early headlines, going out in 33 and staging a familiar last-day charge. Irwin plugged along in his wake, playing level par over the front nine but, as often happens, as Norman's flame fizzled out, Irwin's burst into brilliant, pyrotechnic fire.

He birdied four holes in a row from 11 through 14 and the longest putt he had to make was on the 14th, from 12 feet, such was the quality of his iron play. He had, in the space of 40 minutes, moved from being a top-20 finisher to being a potential champion. He was now seven under par although the leader, Donald, was two strokes ahead

but yet to play the back nine. Irwin estimated that Donald was likely to drop at least one stroke coming home so he therefore needed another birdie himself to get to eight under par and have the chance of a playoff, if not the title itself.

Despite this knowledge, Irwin missed birdies at 16 and 17 (from eight and 12 feet respectively) and consequently stalked his putt on the 18th believing that it had to go in. It was 45 feet long, broke four feet from the right and one observer timed the ball taking over seven seconds to reach the cup.

Hoewever, when it got there the galleries and Irwin erupted. This normally unemotional, thoughtful man was suddenly galloping around the green as if he had already won – and the championship leaders still had nine holes to go.

Extra time

Irwin had been there before and he knew how tough it is to win the US Open. He also began to savour, for the third time, the sweet taste of success. As history showed, Donald hung on to an eight-under-par score and an 18-hole playoff the next day. After those extra holes the two men were still deadlocked but Irwin finally broke Donald's chains, and heart, on the 19th hole with a birdie three. But he, and we, knew that he won the championship on the 18th hole the day before – with that putt.

That old Jones magic

The question: 'Who is the greatest golfer who ever lived?' is as academic as it is pointless. Although it is great fun to imagine Jack Nicklaus in competition against Ben Hogan, or how those masters of matchplay Seve Ballesteros and Walter Hagen would have fared against each other, all that any of these supremely gifted golfers can do is beat their contemporaries.

In these terms there has never been a better golfer than Bobby Jones. Consider the evidence: he played in 11 US Opens; won four and was runner-up the same number of times; he played four Opens, did not complete the first (having torn up his score card in disgust) and won the other three; he won one out of three British Amateur titles and won the US Amateur titles five times (also being beaten finalist twice and beaten semi-finalist twice). In seven years between 1923 and 1930 he played in 21 majors and won 13 of them.

Achieving the impossible

But of all those records, one stands out above all others. In 1930, the year of his retirement at the age of 28, Jones completed the old Grand Slam, a feat that, it can be asserted with a fair degree of confidence, will never be equalled.

During that momentous year, it was probably the US Open, held at Interlachen, Minneapolis, that gave Jones the hardest time. He had, admittedly, needed to play 19 holes of the British Amateur against Cyril Tolley but the competition was the first of the big four and therefore the pressure could not have been considered so great.

Faltering steps

By the time Jones reached Interlachen, he was halfway to his dream, yet had already announced that he had played his last Open Championship. Therefore he, and the world, knew that if the 'Impregnable Quadrilateral', as Jones called it, was to be won, this would have to be the year.

He played steady golf over the first two days and then emerged to shoot a graceful 68 on the third, opening up a five-stroke lead. Many would have considered this a safe margin for a man of Jones' calibre but he was always tormented by nerves and was known to be physically sick when the pressure mounted. This was demonstrated over the opening holes of the final day when his loose play allowed his pursuers to close within a stroke. Jones then rallied but over the last few holes was being hounded by Macdonald Smith, so the American arrived at the 18th believing he needed a birdie for victory.

The putt was 40 feet long, uphill and with a significant break but Jones struck his final stroke ever in the US Open with a confidence that belied the fragile state of his exposed nerves. He holed it with apparent ease, won the championship by two strokes and went on to take the US Amateur at a canter a few weeks later.

CHAPTER EIGHT

Why should putting be difficult?

by Craig DeFoy

When a golf ball is struck with a full swing, the club head travels a substantial distance at high speed. To create a successful shot, the club face must meet the ball at impact perfectly square to the target and on the correct swing path. Furthermore, the ball must be struck in the very centre of the club face – the sweet spot – whilst travelling at speeds of up to 120mph if the blow is to be a true and powerful one.

The level of technical ability needed to perform such a swing is very high, as is the coordination of hand and eye. A good sense of balance and smooth rhythm are also essential, so it is hardly surprising that the 'perfect' shot is so elusive.

A putt on the other hand requires only a relatively small movement of the club head, so the technique is comparatively simple. An elderly lady is just as capable of sinking a long putt as a fit young man, so neither is strength a requirement.

Therefore, to strike a ball towards the hole with a putter would appear to be a fairly undemanding exercise; why then do all golfers of whatever handicap struggle to putt consistently well?

Why should putting be difficult?

The ultimate shot

The putt is the ultimate stroke in golf, for unless a poor drive or approach shot can be redeemed by a good recovery shot, the putt is your last resort; if it misses the hole, there is no redemption – the stroke has been finally lost! This creates an added pressure in putting, and pressure is the last thing you need if you are going to play good golf. This special pressure to succeed manifests itself in many ways, from just inconsistent results to the dreaded 'yips'. No-one is exempt from putting problems; not the ordinary club golfer nor even some of the finest players in the history of the game. Even the legendary Ben Hogan is said to have suffered from the 'yips' towards the end of his career, and, more recently, great players such as Tom Watson and, very prominently, Bernhard Langer have struggled to reproduce their earlier form on the greens. It is generally accepted in the professional ranks that the first part of a player's game to go into decline is the putting – surprising perhaps when we consider that our physical abilities decline with age. The pressure of competition for vast amounts of prize money must obviously affect the golf professional but surely the average club player should not be affected by nerves or tension? Or should they? Millions of golfers around the world would probably be prepared to argue that point.

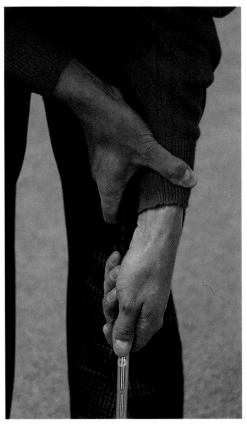

Bernhard Langer holds the putter shaft against his forearm to create a firmer and much more positive putting movement. This adjustment to his putting grip has helped him to overcome the 'yips' and regain his former form.

What is required?

If putting requires neither strength nor a particular complex technique, what attributes or skills are needed? Good putting is a matter of touch and confidence allied to a method that is easily repeatable. Jack Nicklaus has been a consistently fine putter throughout his long career. In his book *Golf My Way*, Nicklaus describes putting as 'two per cent technique and 98 per cent inspiration, or confidence and touch – the only thing great putters have in common is touch, and that's the critical ingredient'.

Touch is the ability to roll the ball at the correct speed, but something else is needed to hole putts – the ability to judge the precise line since golf greens are hardly flat!

Good putting therefore is dependent on touch, judgement of speed and line, and good nerves so that we don't succumb to pressure. If these attributes together with a reliable technique are the vital elements of successful putting, then we now need to explore how the state of the golfer's mind affects his or her performance.

What should I think about?

Since good putting has little to do with technique, there is obviously no point in wasting your mental energy worrying about how to stand or what to do with the hands and wrists during the stroke. It is far more important to trust your method and allow your mind to focus on the complex variables of line and length. Since the line of any putt will vary according to the speed at which the ball travels, the permutations are almost endless. A golfer's approach to putting is generally in keeping with his approach to the rest of the game; a naturally attacking player will tend to putt aggressively, going for the back of the hole without too much concern for the return. Likewise, the more careful player will most likely tend to stroke his putts so that the ball tends to die into the hole.

All of the relevant aspects of each putt have to be computed by the player and a decision on the line and strength must be made, always within a time span of a few moments at most. The best

way to do this is to allow the subconscious mind to absorb all of the information and let the body use the club naturally without any conscious effort to putt in a particular way. This method requires a great deal of self trust, yet our subconscious is allowed to make all kinds of decisions daily – many more important than how to hit a putt!

Tip

Imagine that the hole is further away than it really is (as shown by the tee pegs). This positive thought encourages a positive putting stroke.

Why should putting be difficult?

For our minds to come to the correct decision, the input of information has to be correct just as the output from a computer is entirely dependent on how the machine is programmed. To sift and process this information, we need to concentrate but what is concentration and how do we ensure that we do not lose this precious commodity?

How do I concentrate?

Concentration is perhaps best described as the ability to focus your attention on one subject to the exclusion of all others. However, you cannot concentrate effectively simply by furrowing the brow and telling yourself to do so. If a subject proves interesting, it will hold your attention, so you are concentrating naturally. It follows then that to concentrate on a putt, you need to find that putt interesting. There are numerous techniques that can be employed to help you focus your attention whilst studying a putt, but this effectiveness depends on how each of us reacts to the information before us.

Trust yourself

Later we shall outline some of these techniques in detail, but for now try to become more interested with the target by finding something of interest in or around the hole – a different coloured patch of grass for example, or a mark on the hole edge itself. Allowing our minds to become absorbed in these details increases our awareness of the length and line of the putt, which in turn enhances our feel for the stroke.

Trust your judgement and instinct to carry out the putt successfully and don't be overconcerned with technique. Think *where* not *how* and you'll be surprised at how many more putts finish near to the hole or, even better, fall in.

Every golf club has at least one elderly member who is a deadly performer on the greens – notice how they always seem to look comfortable over the ball and despatch it towards the hole with a minimum of fuss. Do you really think they are worried about their method? I doubt it!

The benefit of routine

Since putting is even more subject to pressure than the rest of golf, then it is necessary to use every means at your disposal to overcome this stress. Although every stroke in a round of golf has the same value, there seem to be occasions when one particular shot appears more important than normal. It is at these times that our reactions to pressure betray us. Fear of failure can cause us to rush the shot in our anxiety to get it over with or, conversely, we are tempted to think overlong before playing, and our natural rhythm is lost. The almost inevitable result of this is a poor shot.

At no time is this more likely to happen than when faced with a putt. As the putt is so often your last chance to put things right on a hole, it is easy to succumb to trying too hard to salvage your score and over-try. Equally, following a really good approach shot or recovery to within a short distance of the hole, we are quite often guilty of being too casual or over-confident and

in rushing to tap the ball in, we miss – a severe jolt to the ego and our confidence!

Feeling the weight of the putt. Practise this to get the same strike, same roll and same weight. It is a tremendous practice drill for developing better 'feel'.

These are times when a pre-shot routine becomes invaluable. In an ideal world, we would give every shot an equal amount of preparation and planning and would spend the same amount of time on its execution. In this way, each shot becomes like any other – no more or less important. This applies to

Why should putting be difficult?

putting just as much as to any other shot, and if we study the top professionals, it quickly becomes apparent that they approach every putt in an identical way.

Spend some time on the practice green experimenting with various routines until you find one that suits you best. Now make sure that you go through exactly that same routine on every putt. If you normally have two looks at the hole followed by one practice swing for instance, do not be tempted to vary that in any way – an extra look at the hole is unlikely to help but will serve only to interrupt your normal flow. Whilst it is not always easy, you must stick rigidly to your routine whether playing in an important competition or just a friendly fourball match. Sooner than you might think, you will develop this approach into a habit that can only serve you well in the future.

Use your imagination

The use of imagery in golf teaching has long proved to be highly effective. Not all of us, however, respond in the same way to a given image or instruction. People vary greatly in their response to stimuli, and although we are inclined to use all of our senses when learning, each of us tends to have one dominant learning mode. The vast majority of us react best to either sensory or visual instruction and it is important to know in which category you belong. The suggestions that follow are presented for both categories and you should find that one or two will prove beneficial.

Sensory learning mode

If you are a sensory player, try some of the following suggestions:
1 As you rely primarily on feelings, it is vital that your club should balance correctly in your hands so that you can sense accurately the exact amount of energy to put to your stroke. This is almost impossible if you hold the club too tightly yet that will almost certainly be your first reaction when faced with a pressure putt. To relieve the tension in your hands and forearms, first hold the club as tightly as possible, then completely relax. Which feels better? Experiment by holding the putter with different levels of tightness, perhaps working on a scale of 1-10, and find the grip strength that feels and works best for you.
2 For the sensory player, comfort is everything. If you force yourself to stand in a certain way because you think it might be correct then you are unlikely to be successful. Again, experiment to find a stance or an address position that *feels* natural; in this way, the feedback you receive from your muscles will be good, and you are best placed to perform at your peak. Don't worry about looking correct – just feel comfortable!

3 Try 'blind putting'. This might sound extreme, but if you practise putting with your eyes closed then you will become much more

conscious of the feel of your stroke. Line up to a hole, close your eyes and stroke the ball. Now try to estimate where the ball has finished in relation to your target. Doing this for a prolonged period, especially with the help of a friend, will rapidly increase your awareness of your hands and the position of the club face at impact. The more you can develop this awareness of the relationship between your hands and your club face, the better you will putt. With a little practice, you will be surprised at how effectively you are able to putt without looking at the ball. This is a practice drill and not recommended for competitive play, but try it by all means during a friendly round, and note how your all-important *feel* improves.

4 Try a few practice sessions when you look at the hole rather than the ball. This does make a certain amount of sense since if you are already looking at the target, you will be far less likely to move your head and body during the stroke, which is a common cause of missed putts. However, the benefit lies mainly in further increasing your awareness of how your club and body feel during the stroke.

5 Experiment with the length of your backswing for various distances of putts, and discover what feels best for you. Remember that it is essential to accelerate the club head through impact, so the length of your backswing must reflect this – too short and your strike will be 'snatching', too long and the putter will tend to slow down.

6 Always ensure that if you take a practice swing before a putt, it should relate directly to the length of the putt itself. If you have a 10-foot putt, make a practice stroke for that distance and try to reproduce the feel of that stroke exactly when striking the ball.

Why should putting be difficult?

Visual learning mode

Now for the golfers whose main learning mode is visual, here are a few techniques, one or two of which could well prove useful:

1 Study your putting stroke in a mirror or, better still, on video. In this way you will readily see whether your stroke is smooth and unhurried and if the putter head is accelerating through the ball. It is also useful to check up on your alignment because if you are not aiming the putter correctly at the target then you will have to compensate for that during the stroke, which surely must cause inconsistency. Look at your address position and take note of the angle of the club shaft – are your hands level with the ball or too far forward or back? The more you familiarize yourself with the look of your own putting action, the easier it will be to cure any problems that may crop up from time to time.

2 When trying to work out the strength of a putt, certainly from a medium to long range, walk along the line to a position about halfway between the ball and the hole; try a couple of practice strokes from there and see if it helps you to judge the distance better. Dividing the length of a putt into equal segments like this can often be of great benefit to a visual player.

On this putt of about eight feet, the player is taking substantial seven to eight inches borrow. Try to visualize the line from the ball to the hole.

3 A putt with a substantial borrow can be particularly difficult to read, so try imagining a paint or chalk line all the way from the ball into the hole, and visualize your ball travelling along it. Clear visual images like this rather than a vague aim left or right of target can only be of benefit. Like all other practice techniques, this will also require regular practice, but do always remember that the clearer your mental picture of what you are trying to achieve, the greater your chance of holing putts regularly.

Why should putting be difficult?

4 On short putts, select a spot only a couple of inches in front of the ball and on the line of your putt. Now instead of trying to steer the ball a few feet to its target, simply concentrate on rolling it over your chosen spot. Striking the ball solidly for the first few inches along the correct line will almost guarantee that you will hole out more consistently from short range. Most short putts are missed through anxiety, so try to achieve something that you can succeed at readily – putting straight for only a few inches does not seem too difficult does it?

5 Downhill or particularly fast putts can often be very tricky to judge. Imagining that the hole is somewhat nearer than it actually is can help you to strike the putts

You should concentrate not only on rolling the ball over your chosen spot but moving the putter head also over that spot, giving you a positive and smooth putting action.

more correctly. Aim to hit the ball at normal strength to a point along the line rather than striking it more gently. The mental picture so produced will make it much easier for you to gauge the level of energy needed to get the ball consistently closer to the hole.

Imagery

Some of the best mental devices to raise a golfer's confidence involve the use of imagery. Seeing the hole as being much bigger than it actually is can really help your efforts to get the ball close or actually into the hole. Imagine that the hole is not a golf hole at all but just a black hole or void that is capable of sucking up any object that comes within its gravitational field.

Think of how the bath water is sucked down the plug hole, and just imagine how much easier putting would be if the hole had the same effect.

Try it and see – sometimes the most bizarre images can prove to be just the secret that makes all the difference. After all, what do you have to lose? Use your imagination freely and you may well be pleasantly surprised. The way in which we perceive anything in life must be totally different for each individual, so why should golf be any exception?

Why should putting be difficult?

Practice under pressure

Learning to putt consistently well, especially in a competitive environment, is a skill like any other – it requires practice. Practising under stress-free conditions, however, is only of limited value. We must learn to *perform* under pressure. it is only sensible therefore to try to create a pressure situation within which you can practise your putting. Devise a putting practice drill that demands that you hole a number of putts successively and you will soon see how the stress factor increases. For example, take some balls to a position about five paces from the hole, and putt until you can hole three in succession. Hole five in succession from, say, three paces away, then ten in a row from about five feet. Culminate with twenty holed successively from two or three feet. This drill will have you pulling your hair out with frustration, but if you repeat it frequently enough you will soon see an improvement in your ability to cope with the inevitable setbacks when a putt misses and in your ability to cope with a pressure putt on the golf course when it really matters.

Practise putting in a circular pattern around a hole to give you the same strength of putt. The discipline is to concentrate on the different lines you get from different angles.

136

The most important rule

One thing that can be said with certainty about human beings is that we all want to be right. This in-built desire to be seen to be correct can turn into a serious liability if we are not careful.

If you habitually own up to having a putting problem – that is exactly what you will have. Even though nobody wants to putt badly, the golfer who says he is a bad putter will perversely almost always find a way to be just that. Even on a good day for such a player, the putts that go in are referred to as 'lucky' or 'unusual'.

It is absolutely vital to avoid this trap. Good putters always think of themselves as good putters, and the bad days on the greens are considered to be just that – an occasional blemish perhaps.

Even players who struggle with their putting can go a long way towards improvement if they remember this golden rule: never say *'I am a bad putter'*. You can say that on a given day your putting was not up to scratch, but never utter those words. Get into the habit today of saying to yourself *'I am a good putter'*. The more often you reinforce your self-belief with these words, the quicker you will see an improvement.

Summary

Remember – you will be what you say you are so be very careful with your description of your own abilities. The words themselves are not a magic potion, but self-belief is essential for good putting so keep your confidence high by telling yourself that you can succeed: *'I am a good putter!'*

CHAPTER NINE

Practise your putting

by Kevin Jones

O ver the years I have had no difficulty in making golfers understand the importance of putting, but getting them to practise it is the hardest thing. If you watch the top professionals practising before a tournament, 50 per cent of their practice time will be spent on the putting green. If you would like to improve your scores, then you must do likewise. Here are some exercises and drills that will make your practice more rewarding and enjoyable.

Tee peg exercise

You should practise hitting balls at a tee peg to increase the precision of your putting action as shown below. The thinking behind this exercise is that if you can hit the tee peg, then the hole is as big as a bucket! Try varying the length of the putts, starting from three feet away and then gradually moving further away, still putting to the tee peg each time to increase your putting precision.

Practise your putting

The two 'D's

There are two problems that we can overcome with practice, and they are what I call the two 'D's – *Distance* and *Direction*. First we will work on *Direction*. To get proper direction, the club must swing along the ball-to-target line, and the club face must be at right angles to the target line at impact with the ball.

To help you do this, get a piece of wood two inches thick by four inches wide and about three feet long. Draw a line in the middle of the wood at right angles to the length. Place the wood on a flat piece of green or carpet, so that the line is about one foot from the hole. Rest the heel of the putter head against the wood and opposite the line, using the line to help you square the putter face. Now let the putter swing back and through with the heel against the wood at all times. This will ensure that the club is travelling on the ball-to-target line. After a few swings without a ball, place a ball opposite the line on the wood so that it is in the centre of the putter. Now use the same putting stroke as before and repeat several times – when the ball goes into the hole you have *Direction*. The club head is swinging on the target line and the club face is at right angles to the target line at impact. After many successful attempts, pull the wood back to two feet and then to three feet. Do not use the wood on longer distances as the club head will begin naturally to swing on the inside of the target line. Now stand away from the wood and, with no ball and eyes

closed, practise the stroke – you should be able to 'feel' the swing path. Open your eyes and repeat. Now go back to one foot from the hole, and hole three balls, then move to two feet and three feet.

Keep going back to your piece of wood to get the correct feel. This piece of wood will become a useful practice aid and should be used to help you line your feet correctly when hitting long shots on the driving range.

140

Chalk line

Many tournament professionals carry a builder's chalk line to make a chalk line on the green about four feet long from the centre of the hole. Then they putt along the chalk line checking that the club face is at right angles to it. This exercise should take place on a flat piece of green, and the chalk line will do no harm to the green.

Take a piece of string four feet long, and tie each end to a long tee peg. Place one tee peg just past the hole and run the string over the edge of the hole to four feet. Place the toe of the putter head against the string so that you can see a right angle with the club face, and play a few putts.

Hold the finished position

Using your piece of wood, string, chalk line or club, strike a ball from three feet and hold the finished position to check that the club face is still square to the target line. This is a good habit to get into as it will tell you if the ball has missed to the left or right because of the break on the green or because the club face was not at right angles to the target line at impact.

Practise your putting

Direction and break

Pick a spot on the green that gives you a 12-foot long breaking putt, either right to left or left to right. Place six balls in a straight line, the first two feet from the hole, the others at two-foot intervals. Play the first putt straight – the majority of putts from two feet from the hole are straight. Continue to play the other five putts straight at the hole and observe the curve the ball makes at the hole. The last three putts will miss if you have hit them straight at the hole because of the break in the green.

Line up another six balls and start again with the knowledge of how the green breaks. As you approach the fourth ball, you will most probably have to aim outside the hole to allow for the break, and further outside for the fifth and sixth putts.

Stand back and try to identify where the break comes from. Look for the high point around the hole; the ball will break from the high point to the low point. This exercise will help you to realise why a ball often moves in a curve on the green.

Spot putting

Position a ball three feet from the hole, and place a ball marker or small coin six inches in front of the ball directly on the line to the hole. Line the putter face up with the marker, then the hole, and stroke the ball over the marker and into the hole. It is easier to aim the putter face to a spot six inches away than one that is 35 feet away. As your confidence increases with this exercise, move further away but keep placing a marker six inches in front of the ball.

Now try without a marker but look for something six inches in front of the ball to aim over. It may be a blade of grass, an old pitch mark or spike mark or just a different coloured blade of grass – there is always something there. This method is especially effective with putts that have a great break to them. It is difficult to aim the ball six feet right of the hole, so imagine the curve the ball will take, pick a spot six inches in front of the ball and line up on that spot, never looking at the hole.

Distance method

This method of practice will help you to understand how the length of the stroke affects the distance the ball will run. Take a few practice swings with your eyes closed and feel how your hands move backwards and forwards. Now let your hands swing back to what feels like three inches to you, and forwards three inches past where the ball should be. Therefore the forward stroke is six inches long. Still with your eyes closed, swing back and through saying to yourself, "Three inches back, three inches through," visualizing the stroke with the ball. Take four balls, with your eyes open, stroke to no particular target, using the same pace of stroke for each ball and saying to yourself, "Three inches back, three inches through." Continue to practise until you can cluster the balls in a circle of one-foot diameter. Pace this distance out. The balls may have run two paces. Now with a stroke six inches back and six inches through, repeat the exercise until you can cluster the balls in a circle one yard in diameter. Pace the distance the balls have run. Continue with strokes of nine, 11, 12 and 18 inches until you have a chart in your mind that may read like this:

Hands move back:	and past the ball	the ball runs
3 inches	3 inches	2 paces
6 inches	6 inches	4 paces
9 inches	9 inches	6 paces
12 inches	12 inches	6 paces
15 inches	15 inches	10 paces
18 inches	18 inches	12 paces

Everybody's chart will be slightly different depending on the natural pace at which they swing the putter.

143

Practise your putting

The benefit of this exercise will be revealed when you are playing the course. Pace the putt – if you are 10 paces away on a flat green, you use a 15-inch swing. It will help when you play different golf courses to quickly discover the pace of new greens. Spend 10 minutes on their practice putting greens to see how your chart compares with their greens and adjust accordingly.

To help feel distance

Place four balls on the green. Putt the first ball along the green at no particular target. Watch the ball run and try to feel the pace of the stroke you have just used. Now putt the other three balls, trying to finish as close to the first ball as possible. Repeat this several times, always watching and feeling. Then carry out the exercise without looking up to watch the ball run. Ask yourself whether you strike the ball in the same way? Did the speed feel the same? Is it short or long? Left or right? Did it sound the same? Off-centre strikes will not run as far.

1st ball Strike at no particular target; watch, study and feel.

2nd ball Strike; do not look up. Ask yourself is it near to the ball? Your answer might be: 'It felt a faster stroke'. The ball is two yards past and to the left. Have a look – are you correct?

3rd ball Strike. Do not look up. Ask the questions: long, short, right or left? Answer: the sound was wrong so the ball is three yards short but straight. Look up; are you correct?

4th ball Repeat.

This is an exercise that will prompt you to ask yourself the correct questions and help you to build a library of feel.

Distance pennies

This is a game we used to play at school with pennies. Throw a penny towards a wall, and the penny nearest to the wall that has not touched it wins.

Start with some balls three feet from the apron of the green. Stroke the balls to the apron – they must not touch or roll over the apron. If this happens, bring the balls back and start again. Gradually move further and further away. While you are practising this exercise, you should be thinking only of distance and of how hard to hit the ball; this will help to create that elusive quality in golf called *feel*.

Look at the hole

Start from three feet away. Address the ball and aim the putter face, looking at the hole. Continue looking at the hole as you swing the putter towards it. This will help to make you aware of the hole and target line, and stops you becoming transfixed on the ball. You are more likely to stroke through the ball instead of hitting at it or stopping at the ball. This exercise will also make you aware of direction and target line and is a great way to putt if you are consistently missing those short putts. Vary the distances where you practise.

Practise your putting

Training the right side: Elephant's trunk

Address the ball, holding the club only in your right hand. Bring the left arm forwards and to the right so that it hangs covering the shaft but not touching anything. This position of the left arm will encourage correct shoulder alignment. Swing the putter and strike through the ball. The left arm must *not* move. You will be swinging the right arm under the left arm, and if you keep the left arm in this position it will help to eliminate unnecessary body movement. On the follow through, check that the putter face is square to the target line and if this is the case, you have just felt the correct right-side release. Try to cluster the balls in a circle of one yard in diameter. This exercise helps to promote the correct use of the right hand and arm and allows you to feel the correct release of the putter head.

Training the left side

This exercise helps promote the correct use of the left hand, wrist, arm and shoulder. Take up your address position with only your left hand holding the putter. Place your right hand on the back of your right thigh to encourage the correct shoulder alignment, which should be square to the target line. Make a stroke with the left hand, leaving the right hand on your thigh. As you follow through, hold the follow-through position so that you can check that the club face is square to the target line.

Play six balls, trying to cluster them together in a circle one yard in diameter. Once you can cluster the balls together you will begin to feel that the left side has to pull. If you are having trouble clustering the balls, your left wrist is hinging on the forward swing; this always leads to inconsistent distance and accuracy.

Connection

To help connect the arms, hands and shoulders so that they are all working together, place a golf club underneath your upper arms with the grip end pointing towards the hole. Address the ball and feel that the shaft is parallel to the ball-to-target line. Make a stroke with the shaft in place and hold the follow through. Check to see where the shaft is pointing. If the shaft is pointing to the left of where it started, you have rotated your shoulders too much and will have pulled the ball left of the hole. However, if the shaft is pointing right of where it started, you have dropped your right shoulder and will have pushed the ball to the right. This exercise will help you to feel squareness and a connection between the arms, shoulders and hands.

Practise your putting

Tension scale 1 to 10

Hold the putter as tight as you can. Feel your thumbs, hands, forearms, biceps and shoulders tighten. This represents 10 on your tension scale, and you should never feel like this in any golf shot. Identify this feeling, as it destroys all golf shots, especially putting. Now loosen your grip so that the putter twists in your hand; this is a 1 on your tension scale. This is of no use because the putter would twist in your hand as you made contact with the ball. You need to be holding the club ideally between 3 and 6 on the scale. Each individual will have their own tension scale. Practise this exercise to identify the tension that will suit your stroke. Learn to identify all 10 grips as you will have this feeling many times throughout a round of golf. It will destroy your game if you do not dispel it immediately.

Clockwork putting

Place six balls around the hole two feet away, and move around, holing these putts. If you miss, start again with all six balls. When you have holed six balls on the trot, move to three feet away, repeat and see how far away you can get from the hole. This will break up the monotony of practice putting and add a competitive element to your practice. It will also show you that around the hole there is a different line and pace for each putt. They may be uphill, downhill, left-to-right or right-to-left breaks.

Putting

Head still and listen

Start with the balls one foot from the hole. Aim the club face, close your eyes, make a stroke and listen to the ball dropping into the hole. When you have had some success, move further away and repeat. Can you feel how the putter swings and gathers the ball? Because you do not know where the ball is you cannot hit at the ball or stop your follow through short. Your head has to stay still or you could miss the ball altogether, and you are training yourself to listen to it dropping into the cup.

Striped ball

Use a felt-tip pen and mark a ring around the circumference of the ball.

1 Place the ball with the stripe horizontal to the green to try to give the feeling that you are applying topspin.

2 Line the stripe up with a hole; this will help you with direction. As the ball runs, the stripe will show if you have struck the ball square.

3 Aim the print of the manufacturer's name up with the hole.

Progression

Start with one ball one foot from the hole. Each time you hole the ball, move back six inches on the same line. See how far away you can get from the hole – back to the beginning if you miss. This will help your concentration and will bring a competitive element to your practice.

Pace

Find a putt five or six feet long with a definite break. Feel how many different speeds you can use to roll the ball into the hole.

Fast   You can hit the ball straight

Medium You aim to the right lip of the hole

Slow   You aim two inches outside the right lip of the hole

CHAPTER TEN

Putting tips from the pros

O n the next few pages you will find some useful putting tips from the professionals which you can try out to help perfect your putting action. Some of the important Rules of Golf relating to putting are also featured, which are useful to know in certain situations you may encounter on the greens. And there are tips and advice on remedying some common putting faults.

Using a sand wedge from the fringe

Sometimes when you are playing from against the fringe of the green, it is preferable to use the leading edge of a sand wedge instead of your putter. Line it up with the equator of the ball to avoid snagging the grass on the backswing. Being careful to keep your wrists firm, swing the club back and try to create some topspin by striking the ball just above or on its equator. This is the shot used by the pros and if it is good enough for them, you should try to perfect it too. But remember that the stroke is a putting stroke – not a pitch. The bottom edge of the sand iron gives it the necessary weight to travel through the rough grass prior to the ball without getting snagged.

Putting tips from the pros

Hands too far back

Here the hands are too far back behind the ball and the player has lost the angles he created at address. The left arm has buckled and gone towards the hole, the wrist action has become excessive, and the blade is hooded as the club head is taken back. To try to recover, the left wrist has broken and the right hand is giving a scooping movement to the ball. In other words, from an incorrect position at address, everything you look for in a putting motion has been destroyed.

Missing short putts

If you regularly miss two- and three-foot putts, then your putting technique needs improving and you may need to employ a firmer wrist action. Using the reverse overlap grip will help (if you don't already do so) as this helps you to maintain a firmer left wrist and gives you more control over the putter. Try the following practice drill to help you build a consistent technique that really works. Just lay down two parallel clubs on the putting surface to create a track through which the ball must pass to the hole – about two feet away. Now practise putting the ball along this track. Persevere and you should soon develop a sound technique which will make you feel more confident on the greens.

Putting tips from the pros

Steering the ball

Above and right: These are good positions to adopt. We all know the golden rule of keeping the head still when putting.

This is a common fault and, as you will find to your cost, if you try to guide the ball into the hole on short putts, you will almost inevitably miss. This is because you will move your upper body and head too much, thereby causing the ball to go wide of the target. Instead, you should choose a point on your selected line just a few inches past the ball and then concentrate on rolling the ball over it, rather than steering the ball into the hole.

Right: The player has tried to keep his head still but he has moved his shoulders and upper body away from the ball, whereas this must be the most stable part of your putting action.

Putting tips from the pros

Downhill putts on links courses

The putting greens on many links courses are larger than inland ones and you should try to get as close to the hole as you possibly can. On these greens, pace is usually more important than borrow, particularly on tricky downhill putts. To avoid hitting the ball off-line or over-hitting or under-hitting, you could try addressing it with it positioned more towards the toe of the putter rather than on the sweet spot, which is the normal position with the blade of the club square and grounded. This has the effect of making the blade slower and the ball come off the club face slightly more slowly at impact but still with a positive strike. However, you should not address the ball with the neck of the club. This is an unreliable method which tends to turn the blade of the club, and it is not recommended.

Above: This is a good position with the blade of the club square and grounded, and the ball in the centre on the sweet spot. Above right: This is the set up for putting on very fast downhill greens. It makes the blade slower but still creates a positive strike. Right: Here the ball is addressed on the neck of the club – a very unreliable way of addressing the ball. This will tend to turn the blade of the club and is not recommended.

Putting

Marking the ball

You should mark the ball when your ball is in the line of your partner or opponent. Your ball is required to be marked, on this occasion, to the right of your partner's ball. Therefore you approach the ball from the right. Place a marking disc directly behind the ball and then take your ball away. Now place the toe of your putter behind the marker, and place another marker at the heel of the putter. You then remove the forward marker so that the line for your partner is clear. If your partner requires further distance, the same procedure of putting toe and then heel to marker two or three putters' lengths if required, can be followed. However, do remember to put your one, two or three club lengths back again when you re-spot the ball.

Removing an obstruction

Here we have a situation where the ball has lodged against a loose impediment on the green, in this case a chocolate wrapper. The marker or disc is placed directly behind the ball, the ball is lifted, the wrapper removed, and the ball is replaced in front of the marker.

Index

Numbers in *italics* refer to illustrations.

158

Putting

Index

Golf books from Collins Willow

The Golf Swing	David Leadbetter
The Golf World Guide to Better Golf	Golf World
Improve Your Golf	Golf World
Psycho Golf	Dr Willy Pasini
Starting Out in Golf	PGA Professionals
The Sunday Telegraph Golf Course Guide	Donald Steel